The Genius of Fear

Unlocking Hitchcock's Cinematic Secrets

by Johnathan Harvey

Formatted, Converted, and Distributed by eBookIt.com
http://www.eBookIt.com

ISBN-13: (hardcover)
ISBN-13: 9781456641856 (paperback)
ISBN-13: 9781456641849 (ebook)
ISBN-13: 9781456641863 (audiobook)

Dear Esteemed Reader,

Thank you immensely for choosing this book to join your collection. We imagine that you've already embarked on an exploration of ideas within these pages, and we couldn't be happier about it!

Now, if you find yourself chuckling, pondering, or even debating with the words in front of you, we'd absolutely love to hear about it. If you can spare a few moments to pen down your thoughts in a review, we would be as delighted as a dictionary on a spelling bee!

An Amazon review would be excellent - but hey, we're far from picky. Whether it's a scribble on the back of a grocery list, a tweet, or even a message in a bottle (though that might take a while to reach us), your feedback is gold.

Writing a review might not be as fun as a spontaneous dance-off, but we promise it'll bring grins to our faces, warmth to our hearts, and incredibly valuable insights to future readers.

With Gratitude,

Bo Bennett, PhD
Publisher
Archieboy Holdings, LLC.

Table of Contents

Introduction

Welcome to the captivating and suspense-filled world of Alfred Hitchcock, one of cinema's most vibrant and influential figures. This book presents an in-depth analysis of the man behind the camera, the genius who weaved together elements of cinematography to create film masterpieces. Delving into the complexities of Hitchcock's unique style, you'll find an exploration of the cinematic elements enhancing the immersive and thought-provoking narratives that have enthralled audiences for decades. This bears testimony to not just the art of filmmaking, but also how it's been masterfully employed by Hitchcock to convey suspense, drama, and plot twists. This book isn't just about understanding Hitchcock, it's about extracting nuances from within his work that can be celebrated by movie buffs, studied by film students, or imitated by aspiring filmmakers. On this cinematically dramatic adventure, you'll discover how Hitchcock, using light, camera angles and movement, visual effects and sound, transformed ordinary scenes into extraordinary ones; turning the mundane into the magnificent. This book doesn't just aim to deconstruct Hitchcock's cinematic universe, but also to provide a foundation that can enhance your passion for, or understanding, that is filmmaking.

The Legacy of Alfred Hitchcock

Hitchcock's legacy is woven into the very fabric of modern cinema, enduring through the decades with an unabating influence on emerging filmmakers, critics, and audiences alike. By pushing the boundaries of traditional filmmaking techniques and genres, Hitchcock established himself as a pioneering force in cinema, continually challenging and evolving his craft, and ultimately the art of storytelling itself.

His impact goes far beyond the individual elements of his films; Hitchcock's ideas have shaped the film industry and popular culture in profound ways. His name has become synonymous with suspense, terror, and psychological intrigue, signifying an entire subset of cinema that he virtually birthed — a fitting testament to the lasting power of his films and their impact on the cultural psyche.

Hitchcock's approach of placing ordinary people in extraordinary circumstances became a genre unto itself, forging a new path in cinema's narrative landscape. He was inventive, audacious, and fearlessly experimental, masterfully using every tool and technique available to him to pull viewers deep inside the minds and fears of his characters. That emotional journey Hitchcock took audiences on is a testament to his genius and a key element of his enduring legacy.

Hitchcock's prowess was not limited to suspense and fear, but extended to a profound understanding of the human psyche and its complexities. An important part of his legacy lies in the intricate character portraits he crafted, their psychological depth revealed through subtle cinematic motifs and visual cues. His films remain some of the finest examples of character study and psychological dissection, leaving imprints on viewers' minds long after the movie's end.

One of Hitchcock's most admired techniques was his use of the camera to engage and manipulate the audience. He would orchestrate the film too, not just show it, to elicit the emotions he desired. He created suspense not by what he showed but by what he did not, often leaving the most horrifying scenes to the viewers' imagination. The legacy of this technique can be seen in countless films and television shows today, demonstrating its enduring influence.

The 'Hitchcock blonde' is another testament to the director's pervasive influence. His fondness for cool, aloof, and attractive blondes became one of his trademarks, forever aestheticizing a certain archetype alongside the intense suspense and psychological drama that defined his signature style.

Even in aspects of film often overlooked by other directors, such as sound design, Hitchcock was a trendsetter. He effectively used the interplay of sound and silence, music and noise, to heighten the suspense and terror in his films. The powerful, haunting score of 'Psycho' is a prime example of Hitchcock's innovative use of sound, which continues to influence the industry to this day.

Furthermore, Hitchcock's influence extended beyond the silver screen to redefine the role and image of the director. He was ubiquitous, often appearing in cameos in his films, and starring in televised introductions to his television series, Alfred Hitchcock Presents. This cultivated a cult of personality around him, turning the director into a celebrity icon—a phenomenon that has become commonplace today.

Hitchcock's legacy in the realm of commercial success cannot be ignored either. At a time when the financial success of movies was often at odds with artistic ambition, Hitchcock managed to straddle worlds, delivering box-office successes without compromising his creative vision. This too is part of his legacy, paving the way for future auteurs who aspire to commercial success without artistic compromise.

Alfred Hitchcock may have been known for his suspense, but it's clear that his powerful influence extends beyond any one genre. His innovative techniques, combined with his keen understanding of the human experience, have left an indelible mark on cinema and popular culture alike. He revolutionized the film industry, reshaped narratives, and redefined our relationship with fear in ways that continue to influence filmmakers and captivate audiences today.

His films, with their stunning visuals, sophisticated narratives, and profound psychological insights, have stood the test of time, their innovative techniques battling obsolescence, and their impact echoing in the works of countless contemporary filmmakers. Indeed, there is hardly a thriller or suspense film today that doesn't carry some trace of Hitchcock's influence.

It is fitting, then, that we end the introduction to this book with a nod to the enduring influence of Alfred Hitchcock. Whether you are a budding filmmaker looking to understand and incorporate Hitchcock's techniques, a film student seeking to delve deeper into his craft, or simply an admirer of his work, the journey through Hitchcock's cinematic universe promises to be as thrilling as his films themselves.

In the following chapters, we will delve into the rich layers of Hitchcock's artistry, examining the elements and techniques that made his films so unforgettable. From the unrelenting suspense of 'Psycho' to the mounting dread of 'The Birds,' from the dizzying heights of 'Vertigo' to the voyeuristic thrill of 'Rear Window,' Hitchcock's legacy lives on, pulsating with menace, suspense, and an undying fascination for the depths of the human psyche.

As the pages turn and anticipation builds, we will explore every nook and cranny of Hitchcock's world, from the crimson blood swirling down the drain in 'Psycho' to the looming Mount Rushmore in 'North by Northwest.' There is much to uncover, and every revelation brings us closer to understanding the true genius of Alfred Hitchcock, whose indomitable spirit and innovative vision continue to inspire and captivate us.

Aim and Scope of the Book

The primary aim of this book is to delve beyond the surface-level appreciation of Alfred Hitchcock's legendary films, to explore the unique and innovative cinematic techniques he employed. While Hitchcock's work delights audiences with its narrative complexity and dramatic flair, this book endeavors to shed light on the intricate elements, both visual and auditory, that make his films so distinct and enduring. Hitchcock's eclectic tapestry of work is renowned for its unique cinematography and this endeavor examines these elements keenly, imparting a deeper understanding of his films.

To effectively dissect Hitchcock's films and techniques, this book draws extensively from film theory, visual aesthetics, and Hitchcock's own interviews and writings to create a comprehensive yet digestible guide. The aim is not only to cater to film students, scholars, and creatives interested in the field of filmmaking, but also to appeal to the myriad of avid film enthusiasts who admire Hitchcock's work. This meticulous analysis of Hitchcock's films seeks to enhance their appreciation and understanding of this legendary director's work.

The book's scope spans Hitchcock's filmmaking career, offering in-depth insights into his well-known classics such as "Vertigo", "Psycho", "Rear Window", "North by Northwest" and "The Birds", as well as shedding light on lesser-known gems like "Rope", "Strangers on a Train" and "Dial M for Murder". By scrutinizing these films, the book seeks to demystify Hitchcock's unique and innovative techniques and enable readers to grasp his idiosyncratic style.

The book meticulously analyzes Hitchcock's iconic techniques, such as his innovative use of the camera, his manipulation of light and shadows, his dynamic framings and montage techniques. The text delves into Hitchcock's inventive use of sound and music to create suspense and drama, while offering an appreciation of the importance he placed on visual storytelling. More intricately, the book discusses thematic aspects like symbolism, motifs and the clever use of MacGuffins to maintain engagement.

Furthermore, the book explores the role and contributions of Hitchcock's collaborators, including the actors, actresses, writers, and composers who helped coalesce his visionary work. It acknowledges their collective input and individual talents which significantly augmented the impact of Hitchcock's storylines, performances, and suspenseful scores.

In its latter pages, the book reflects on Hitchcock's enduring influence on modern cinema, particularly his impact on the genre of thrillers. It aims to demonstrate how Hitchcock's films have influenced current filmmakers and how themes and techniques from his films resonate still, cementing his legacy in the enduring fabric of cinematography.

The book distinguishes itself through its heightened focus on the language of cinematography. It consolidates fundamental film theories while illustrating their utilization within Hitchcock's work. This study intends to serve as an invaluable tool for film students and aspiring filmmakers, equipping them with the expertise to explore the language of films critically and creatively.

Structured to facilitate the understanding of key concepts in a sequential manner, the book traces Hitchcock's trajectory from his early breakthrough to his defined later works. This approach ensures an organized exploration of the depth and breadth of Hitchcock's filmography.

The principles and methods discussed, however, go beyond Hitchcock's contribution and provide a strong platform for readers to analyze movies more broadly. In essence, the book uses the works of Hitchcock as a lens through which to describe and explain fundamental film concepts and techniques, making it substantially more than just a compendium of Hitchcock's work.

Ultimately, the book's aim and scope intertwine to paint a vivid picture of the journey behind Hitchcock's most remarkable films. From conceptualization to the technicolor tapestry of the silver screen, you'll gain not just an etched understanding of Hitchcock's works, but also an enriched perspective of movie-making.

In conclusion, this book invites both casual and dedicated film enthusiasts on an immersive journey where the magic of the silver screen is unravelled to reveal the careful thought, technical prowess and individual genius that goes into crafting classic films.

How to Use This Guide

With a distinct premise and structured layout, this guide is designed to let you navigate effortlessly through the brilliance often embedded deeply within Hitchcock's illustrious filmography. Rather than a traditional start-to-finish direction, you might prefer a more exploratory, interest-led approach. You're free to select sections in your desired order based on the specific topic, film, or curiosity you decide to unpack. Whether you're a film enthusiast, a student, or simply someone who loves delving into cinematic universes, this guide is flexible to your preferred pace and sequence.

In each chapter, there's a significant exploration of a characteristic technique, scene, or theme from Hitchcock's works. This structure can help you to sieve out key elements and techniques that have made his films stand the test of time. The sections are designed to be comprehensive, so you can read them individually, but they will make more sense if read in conjunction with each other. Interlacing elements from different parts of the guide will foster a comprehensive understanding of Hitchcock's mastery over cinematic storytelling.

Furthermore, not every chapter needs to be closely scrutinized. If you are more interested in a specific film, such as "Psycho", "Vertigo", or "Rear Window", a focused reading of the corresponding chapter should give you a deeper understanding. Additionally, those aiming to gain a wide understanding of Hitchcock's style, can use the guide extensively to build a broad-based knowledge of his work. Through it, you will discern patterns, identify peculiarities, and gain insights about Hitchcock's effective method of scaring and mystifying his audience.

This guide builds itself around a perfect blend of descriptive and analytical discourse which seamlessly weaves through each topic. However, you're encouraged to apply your own interpretation of Hitchcock's works, background, and personality. This book aims to provide fact-based analysis, but the world of cinema is ripe for discussions, debates, and differing viewpoints. As you navigate through the guide, keep in mind that your perspective matters.

Wrapping up the publication is an appendix featuring a glossary of film terms that you may encounter in this guide. In case a term stumps you or a concept seems nebulous, don't hesitate to turn the pages back to this section. You can also consult the recommended readings and viewings for further development of your understanding. This guide is intended to be more than a book to read once and shelve; it aspires to be a companion for your continuing journey through the thrilling world of Alfred Hitchcock.

Chapter 1: The Master of Suspense

Emerging from an era ripe with potential, Alfred Hitchcock was a pivotal figure who bestowed upon us a campfire with flames of anxiety, uncertainty, and spine-chilling terror. Coming up with a genre of his own, Hitchcock expanded the horizons of cinematic storytelling. A master craftsman who stealthily wove plots with threads of suspense, his distinctive style and influence transformed how films were perceived, leaving a mark synonymous with psychoanalytic storytelling. Hitchcock's early works, while not as acclaimed as his later masterpieces, nonetheless played an instrumental role in shaping his trademark storytelling style. He changed the landscape of mystery and horror films, playing into society's underlying fears, and exploiting common phobias. His art of emotional manipulation and suspenseful storytelling transgressed the norms of conventional cinema, igniting the birth of a genre marked by thrilling plots, unexpected twists, and palpable tension. Hitchcock's films taught us something new about fear; they instilled dread and anxiety beneath the facade of everyday life, showing us that something sinister could lurk within even the most mundane of circumstances. He taught us how to anticipate the worst, even when there was nothing to suggest it, hence earning him the eternal title of 'The Master of Suspense'.

Birth of a Genre

Good films have always inherently carried something that transcends them beyond their realms - a distinct style, a peculiar language. Alfred Hitchcock, popularly referred to as the Master of Suspense, rightfully stood out with these qualities, thereby carving out a genre of his own that made his name synonymous with spine-chilling suspense and psychological thrillers.

Hitchcock's unique style was not an instantaneous phenomenon, but a true testament to his gradual experimentation with novel approaches. The birth of this particular genre can arguably be traced back to his stint at the UFA Studios in Germany, where he was exposed to German Expressionism. This exposure not only helped him incorporate innovative visual techniques into his films but also laid the groundwork for him to create films that were aesthetically pleasing and eerily discomforting at the same time.

However, the quintessential element that set Hitchcock's films apart was his unrelenting interrogation of our subconscious fears. He refined his cinematic approach by drawing out the psychological aspect of suspense, transgressing the supposed boundaries of thrillers. This proved to be instrumental in the birth of a genre that we readily identify today as 'Hitchcockian'.

One of the defining traits of 'Hitchcockian' films is the fuse of suspense and humor. He was well-versed in meticulously blending fright with comic relief, thus making his take on the suspense genre less austere and more accessible. This unique combination amplified viewer immersion, as it serviced not just the thrill-seekers, but also those who craved for a cohesive cinematic experience.

His films, more often than not, functioned on an unreachable dread. He toyed with common perceptions and expectations, often leading the audience down an unpredictable path and catching them off guard with his finessed plot twists and turns. It's such uncertainties and plot surprises that made his films perfectly thrilling, and this can definitely be marked as one of the reasons why his works forged a new genre.

His choice of taking an ordinary protagonist and tossing them into extraordinary, nerve-wracking situations became a popular trend in his films. While this practice wasn't unique to Hitchcock, it was his style of execution that gave it a fresh perspective. His players were not heroes with extraordinary abilities, but everyday humans confronted with the unthinkable. This kind of narrative was a ground-breaking technique that was part of Hitchcock's signature.

Another signature trait of the 'Hitchcockian' genre is the frequent use of the female characters as both an object of desire and a victim, which played into our innate voyeuristic tendencies as viewers. His seminal use of the 'femme fatale' in his films added layers and complexities to his narratives that were typically unseen in the classical detective narratives, further fuelling the birth of his unique genre.

Hitchcock had a knack for making the audience feel trapped, a concept he often implemented on his characters. This trick was usually done through camera angles and close-up shots that created feelings of claustrophobia and anxiety. The way he could bring such feelings to life helped identify and define the 'Hitchcockian' genre.

It was in the stories of ordinary people entangled in extraordinary situations, the fusion of suspense and humor, the perpetual menace grounding his narratives, and the cinematographic manipulation of space and time, that the genre took birth. Hitchcock's films were an amalgamation of his learned ideals, all weaved seamlessly together, giving rise to the birth of a genre that would influence scores of filmmakers in years to come.

The unique blend of Hitchcock's methods, storytelling, and film techniques led to the ascent of a genre identifiable due its idiosyncratic trademarks. Hitchcock's genre birthed innovative possibilities within cinema, while continuing to elevate the standards of narrative storytelling and cinematic aesthetics.

The genre even though cradled in the realm of Hitchcock's films, soon expanded to influence others. Filmmakers and film enthusiasts alike were drawn to Hitchcock's originality. They started adapting and incorporating elements of his cinematic style, rendering an echo to the 'Hitchcockian' genre in their work, thereby prolonging and amplifying its influence.

It's key to note that while Hitchcock didn't invent suspense, he refined it to a groundbreaking level with his intricate contents, unique style, and perception of reality, thereby giving birth to a new genre in which he is yet unmatched.

The birth of this genre wasn't a conscious creation, but rather a unique result of Hitchcock's innovative vision. His undying love for cinema, his unique understanding of the audience's pulse, and his ability to establish and dissolve tension in masterful ways are all elements that danced together to bring to life the unique cinematic species we now associate with his name. This genre's birth is a testament to Hitchcock's ceaseless exploration of cinematic language and his unyielding determination to push the boundaries of traditional storytelling.

To truly appreciate the depth and genius of this genre's birth, we now delve into Hitchcock's style and influence, thereby peeling back the layers of its complex inception and understanding the contributions of this legend to the world of cinema, setting the tone for the masters that are to follow.

Hitchcock's Style and Influence

One cannot speak of the art of suspense in film without the mention of Alfred Hitchcock. He pioneered an insidious style of suspense, intricately woven with a mischievous sense of humor, that has left an indelible mark on the world of cinema.

Every frame of a Hitchcock film was masterfully designed, an assortment of visual symphonies - each serving the grand composition of suspense. His trademark style exemplifies the principle of 'show, don't tell.' The influential filmmaking technique employs careful visuals and sound design, allowing viewers to feel the tension and suspense building rather than having it explained to them. It's in the subtle gestures of the characters, the clever camera movement, the ominous music, and the artful use of colors and shadows. Hitchcock brings out the suspense not just in extraordinary circumstances, but in the mundane as well.

From a technical and stylistic perspective, Hitchcock's work was often characterized by his innovative use of the camera. He had the capacity to construct a scene as though the audience were part of the plot, directly experiencing the psychological states of his characters. This characteristic perspective and his masterful understanding of the human psyche are key elements in his spellbinding suspense.

Hitchcock's trademark camera movement, often described as a "subjective camera," was innovatively used as a storytelling device that involved the viewer directly in the narrative. His camera did not merely record the events, but it played an active role in building tension, often acting as a representation of a character's psychological state.

Furthermore, his unique approach to cinematography was highly innovative, using techniques such as the 'dolly zoom' effect, also known as the 'Vertigo effect,' after its memorable use in the film of the same name. This combined camera move and zoom, which gives the viewer a sense of disorientation and unease, is just one creation in Hitchcock's bag of tricks that has become a staple in modern cinema.

The meticulous director had an extraordinary understanding of the power of sound and music as vital elements of suspense. The shower scene from 'Psycho,' for instance, with Bernard Herrmann's screeching violin score combined with the horrifying visuals, probably holds the crown for the most potent fusion of sound and visuals in a suspense sequence.

Hitchcock was well ahead of his time in experimenting with color grading as well. He fully understood the emotional implications of color and used it masterfully to communicate emotions and feelings. His use of color in 'Vertigo' and the iconic red backdrop in 'Marnie' serve as prime examples of how he connected colors to the psychological states of his characters.

His manipulation of his viewer's anticipation through misdirection is another distinct aspect of Hitchcock's unique movie-making approach. He took great delight in deceiving his audience, often leading them down a path, only to surprise them with an unexpected twist, a trait that has widely been adopted by modern filmmakers.

The presence of 'MacGuffin,' a plot device that took many forms in each of the director's films, was a distinctive attribute of Hitchcock's storytelling technique. Although typically irrelevant to the story's outcome, these elements pushed the plot forward, adding to its bewildering suspense.

Master character development was yet another aspect that made Hitchcock's style distinct and his films memorable. His characters were complex and human, with perfectly imperfect personalities that got tangled in webs of their making, making them relateable to the viewers.

Hitchcock was a trailblazer in using visual metaphors and symbols to convey deeper meanings. He can be called a minimalist poet of motion pictures, who communicated more through his visual language than dialogue. His movies are peppered with symbolisms and metaphoric representations, which often reflected the unconscious motives and desires of his characters.

Hitchcock's enduring style and influence reached far beyond his era. His unique storytelling techniques, mastery of suspense, and pioneering technological approaches have made him an icon whose influence can be seen in films to this day. Filmmakers around the globe continue to study his practices and attempt to replicate his spellbinding suspense.

All these elements combined, they served to elevate Hitchcock's filmmaking style into an elaborate art form, earning him the title of 'Master of Suspense'. His cinematic aesthetics, commitment to detail, storytelling mastery, and his ability to marry visuals with sound set him apart from his contemporaries, making him a true maestro of the cinematic world, whose influence still reverberates throughout the industry.

Summarily, it's enlightening to delve into Hitchcock's overwhelming influence on filmmaking and to recognize how his approach revolutionized cinema. Rest assured, a detailed analysis of Hitchcock's style will provide you with a newfound appreciation of the suspense genre, which has become a mainstay of modern cinema, thanks in large part to his indelible influence.

Early Works and Breakthrough

Alfred Hitchcock began his cinematic journey in the silent era, starting his career as a title designer for silent films in the 1920s. His earliest works, such as "The Pleasure Garden" (1925), showed early glimmers of the director's unique style and talent for suspense. Despite being considered commercially unsuccessful, this film marks the beginning of Hitchcock's interesting and innovative journey in filmmaking.

It was with "The Lodger: A Story of the London Fog" (1927) that Hitchcock first showcased elements of what would become his signature style. The silent thriller, revolving around a series of murders involving young blonde women in London, introduced audiences to Hitchcock's love for suspense and his innovative approach to storytelling. As a long-standing influence on Hitchcock's future work, it is often referred to as "The First Hitchcock film".

Post his silent film successes, Hitchcock transitioned to sound films or "talkies" with "Blackmail" (1929), turning a potential constraint into a compelling narrative device. This film showed Hitchcock's innovative experimentation with sound, a facet that would later become essential in his thrillers, enhancing the underlying tension and suspense.

Throughout the 1930s, Hitchcock continued to innovate and challenge the boundaries of cinema in Britain, directing films like "The Man Who Knew Too Much" (1934), "The 39 Steps" (1935), and "The Lady Vanishes" (1938). These films, innovative in their approach to narrative and suspense, garnered critical acclaim and solidified Hitchcock's reputation as a gifted and innovative filmmaker.

"The 39 Steps", in particular, was a landmark film for Hitchcock. It was here that he introduced one of his recurring plot devices, the "wrong man" theme, where an innocent man is wrongly accused and embarks on a mission to clear his name. This film, heralded for its seamless fusion of comedy and suspense, is often considered one of the finest British films of all time.

A significant turning point in Hitchcock's early career came with his move to the United States in 1939 under the contract with David O. Selznick, an American film producer. Selznick recognized the burgeoning talent and potential in Hitchcock's earlier works and sought him for his next production.

Entering the world of Hollywood with "Rebecca" (1940) - his American debut - Hitchcock won his first (and only) Best Picture Oscar. "Rebecca" is a perfect example of his gothic romantic thrillers, showcasing an intense, eerie atmosphere combined with complex, nuanced characterization. The movie's success truly marked his breakthrough in Hollywood.

Throughout the 1940s and 50s, Hitchcock pushed the boundaries of cinematic storytelling with masterpieces such as "Rope" (1948), "Strangers on a Train" (1951), and "Rear Window" (1954). These films showcased Hitchcock's maturation as a filmmaker, highlighting his exceptional grasp of the cinematic medium and his ability to manipulate it to cultivate tension and excitement.

"Strangers on a Train", one of his most acclaimed works from this period, expertly displays Hitchcock's ability to create a chilling atmosphere. He weaved ordinary characters into extraordinary circumstances, resulting in a suspenseful plot fueled by paranoia and guilt.

"Rear Window", on the other hand, showcased Hitchcock's inclination towards voyeuristic themes, exploring the enthralling and terrifying potential of the visual medium. The unique narrative of a man confined to his room, witnessing a potential murder through his window, was a novel concept and spoke volumes about Hitchcock's innovative storytelling.

In the late 1950s, Hitchcock's career pivoted again with movies like "Vertigo" (1958), "North by Northwest" (1959), and his most successful film, "Psycho" (1960). These films showcased groundbreaking cinematography and innovative storytelling, keeping moviegoers on the edge of their seats.

"Psycho" was arguably the pinnacle of Hitchcock's mainstream success. With its iconic shower scene, it proved that even the simplest storylines could be transformed into nerve-wracking experiences. This revolutionary horror and suspense film is often seen as Hitchcock's finest work and marked a definitive point in his career.

Despite the commercial and critical successes he enjoyed throughout the 1950s and 60s, Hitchcock's career gradually declined in his later years. While his influence can still be seen in numerous contemporary films, it is his early works and his breakthrough period that truly marked Hitchcock's standing in the pantheon of cinema greats.

In conclusion, Hitchcock's early works and breakthrough in Hollywood stand as testament to his creative prowess. His unique voice in filmmaking, combined with a keen understanding of the audience's psyche, gained him both popularity and critical acclaim. Through each of his films, we're offered a masterclass in suspense and tension, elements that have come to define the "Hitchcockian" style. Consequently, Hitchcock continues to inspire countless filmmakers, and his work remains as relevant and thrilling today as it was during his peak.

Chapter 2: The Language of Cinematography

As we delve into the nuanced world of Hitchcock, it's essential to understand the language of cinematography, a primal tool in his storytelling arsenal. This cinematic vernacular, as it were, is composed of key components, each speaking volumes of the narrative, the emotion, and the subtext. Hitchcock's apt use of composition and framing created a distinctive visual syntax, establishing relationships between characters and their environments. It enhanced the emotional impact, whether posing characters within tight spaces to evoke a sense of claustrophobia, or using depth of frame characters to suggest psychological distance. Lighting and shadows furthered these visual articulations, casting characters in obscurity or in stark light to underscore their internal struggles, their secrets, their fears. Hitchcock's pervasive increase in contrast and high key lighting wasn't merely aesthetic, but a stylistic choice to delineate good from evil, reality from illusion. Moreover, sense of movement—through camera angles and positions— brought forth the potency of Hitchcock's visual tales. Innovative techniques such as the dolly zoom manipulated the audience's perception, inducing a sense of unease and tension synonymous with the Master of Suspense. Thus, Hitchcock's astute employment of these attributes, a silent but powerful language, created a cinematic experience unparalleled, sculpting timeless stories shadowed in suspense and mystery.

Composition and Framing

It is impossible to discuss Hitchcock's films without recognizing his unparalleled mastery of composition and framing. In cinematography, it's critical to understand these two primary elements, each laden with potential to dramatically shape the story being told. Hitchcock didn't merely use framing and composition as a passive means of recording a scene, but as a creative tool to enhance suspense, convey subtext, and manipulate the viewer's perspective.

In every film, he planned each shot meticulously. He knew exactly where the camera should be, at what height, and which lens to use. Essential to Hitchcock's style was the concept of the 'Golden Ratio.' This principle, often found in fine art, describes an ideally proportional rectangle, an aspect ratio of 1.618, found often in nature, which is pleasing to the human eye. Hitchcock often applied this 'Rule of Thirds' to his frame composition, positioning important components of a shot along these lines.

Consider the scene from "Psycho" where Marion Crane pulls over to the side of the road to sleep. Hitchcock places Marion's car in the lower third of the shot, the upper two-thirds filled with the vast, darkened landscape, making her vulnerability palpable to viewers.

In "Rear Window," composition and framing played fundamental roles in depicting Jimmy Stewart's immobilized state. Throughout the film, viewers are contained within the small apartment, with a cropping cinematic lens that continuously emphasizes the protagonist's physical limitation and the limited scope of his world view.

Framing these scenes tightly within the apartment windows increased the audience's sensation of voyeurism. Hitchcock's geometry of the set presented the cube of apartments as a stage, with Jeff's apartment acting as the audience's theatre box. Our view is, therefore, directly aligned with the protagonist's.

Hitchcock also employed asymmetrical framing to create visual tension. Scenes are often composed where characters are placed off-center, inciting in the audience a sense of unease or signifying emotional imbalance within a character. This can be seen in "Vertigo," when Scottie is watching Madeleine at the art gallery. The skewed balance helps to deepen the tension and impart a sense of the characters' emotional unsteadiness.

Hitchcock's use of the camera was not passive; every beat and rhythm, every unspoken word were carefully constructed within his frame. He played with perspective and space, used carefully coordinated action to manipulate the viewer's focus, and heightened tension through the careful positioning of characters and objects within the scene.

Take for instance "Psycho's" infamous shower scene. Hitchcock's quick cuts and framing leaves the brutality largely to the audience's imagination. The way he frames Marion Crane, slicing the frame with lines of shadow, makes her vulnerability tangible.

There's also a depth to Hitchcock's composition, a command of the z-axis within his frame. By layering elements within the shot, such as in "North by Northwest" iconic final Mount Rushmore sequence, Hitchcock creates a greater illusion of depth and three-dimensionality. The characters are framed in the foreground, the expansive drop revealed before them, and in turn the audience, heightening the sense of peril.

The famous scene from "The Birds," where the birds gradually gather behind Melanie without her noticing, is another example of Hitchcock's genius. The composition amplifies suspense as Hitchcock refuses to cut away from the shot, causing viewers to anxiously anticipate the inevitable.

Referencing "Vertigo" again, the composition is purposely claustrophobic and closed, mirroring Scottie's obsessive state. Hitchcock crafts scenes with dense compositions, layers of images, busy patterns – all while framing Scottie in the middle, entrapped by his obsession.

On the other hand, take "Rear Window" as an example of open compositions, where multiple points of interest exist within a single frame. The camera deliberately observes the neighbors' lives, portraying their stories simultaneously, creating a rich tapestry of narratives uniquely Hitchcockian in design.

Hitchcock's approach to composition and framing, his vision and creative command over every shot, was instrumental in shaping his films. With each frame, he captured not only the action but also the emotions, tension, and psychological undertones of his narrative, thus making him a true master of visual storytelling.

In conclusion, Hitchcock's mastery of composition and framing stands as a shining example for filmmakers, students, and film lovers to learn from. His landmark innovations continue to influence and inform the world of film, broadening our understanding of what could be achieved within the boundaries of the cinematic frame.

Lighting and Shadows

Hitchcock was a master of storytelling and suspense, and the primary way he expressed these elements of his craft was through his masterful use of lighting and shadows. These inky and atmospheric scenes are a defining part of what makes a Hitchcock movie what it is. By manipulating light and darkness, Hitchcock was able to accentuate the mood of a scene, reveal or obscure the action, and lure the audience into a sense of unease or anticipation.

Let's set the scene with one of his classic films, "Psycho". The infamous shower scene is one of the most iconic instances of Hitchcock's use of light and shadow. The stark contrast of the black-white transitions, the lofty shadows in the room, the harsh glare of the bathroom light collectively elicits an ambiance of terror. It's Hitchcock's bold proclamation that, yes, even in the sanctity of one's bathroom, dread stealthily lurks.

"Vertigo" is yet another compelling testament to Hitchcock's prowess in this area. The gloom that shadows over Scottie's descent into madness becomes more oppressive, the dark corners of the mind become more perilous, and the fearful trepidation of falling adorns an almost tangible form as darkness begins to dominate the lit spaces. As viewers, we are caught in the relentless pull of this disorienting vortex, much like Scottie himself.

Lighting also plays a pivotal role in character portrayal. Hitchcock, famed for his subtle psychology, used the luminary language of lighting to convey implicit character nuances. Tinged with mystery, characters often emerge from shadows or are obscured by them, leaving viewers in a state of anticipation or uncertainty. For example, in "Rope", Brandon and Phillip's faces are repeatedly shadowed, indicating their guilt-hidden malevolence.

Moreover, Hitchcock employed chiaroscuro lighting — a stark contrast between light and dark — to set up a mood of tension and suspense. This is evident in "The Birds", where the erratic lighting tones match the bird attacks' escalating frenzy. The peaceful morning light dwindles into menacing, shadowy twilight, reflecting the town's sinister transformation.

Alfred Hitchcock's work on "Rear Window" showcases a phenomenal use of natural lighting. Hitchcock manipulated different lighting schemes to portray different times of the day accurately, which was not only technically impressive but also used to narrate the cyclical rhythm of city life and the progression of the story.

Shadow, on the other hand, becomes a character in its own right in "Suspicions". As the clouds cast shadows over the landscape and characters, the air pulsates with distrust and looming disaster. Here, shadows are not merely absence of light but ominous markers of underlying tension.

In "North by Northwest", Hitchcock uses shadows to heighten the drama in the sequence where a crop duster plane chases Roger Thornhill. The stark contrasts of the shadow of the plane on the sunlit cornfield amplify the overbearing, relentless menace Thornhill is up against.

Occasionally, Hitchcock also used shadows to hint at plot developments. In "Dial M for Murder", the elongated shadow of the scissors is a covert forewarning of the impending murder, thus maintaining a simmer of suspense throughout.

Looking closely at Hitchcock's collaboration with cinematographers, it's notable to mention the brilliant combination of his and Robert Burks' creativity. Their aligned vision transformed ideas into cinematic reality, as seen in "Strangers on a Train". The shadow of the carousel in the final sequence and the characters' reflection in Bruno's glasses are examples of how light and shadows formed an integral part of the narrative.

Even his less appreciated works like "Marnie" and "The Wrong Man" employs the same meticulous use of heightened contrast to convey suspense and the characters' internal conflicts. Scenes are staged to use light and shadow to relay an emotional impact, stringing the audience along the narrative thread.

Hitchcock's lighting and shadow techniques continued to inspire many thriller and noir filmmakers, foretelling his indelible mark on cinema. The consistent and deliberate use of light and darkness in Hitchcock's movies sheds light (pun intended) on his ingenious ability to induce suspense and drama in his audience, thus solidifying his renown as the 'Master of Suspense'.

So, to reflect on the words of Hitchcock himself: "Drama is life with the dull bits cut out." It becomes evident how lighting and shadows became his sharpest scissors, catalyzing the taut narrative arcs that keep us hanging at the edge of our seats.

In conclusion, Hitchcock's handling of lighting and shadows isn't just about technical proficiency. It's the artful weaving of these elements into the film's fabric, making them as critical to the narrative as any other element. The interplay of light and shadow in Hitchcock's movies goes beyond aesthetic appeal; it becomes a crucial cog in his storytelling mechanism.

Camera Movement and Angles

To truly comprehend the genius of Alfred Hitchcock, studying his use of camera movements and angles serves as a critical starting point. This aspect of cinematography plays a pivotal role in Hitchcock's storytelling, evoking various emotions and suspense like no other director of his caliber.

One particular technique that Hitchcock frequently employed was intricate camera movement. Filmmaker's camera inherently serves as the viewer's eye looking into the film's world. Hitchcock masterfully directed the movements of this 'eye' to guide viewers through his meticulously crafted scenes. By roaming, panning, tilting, or tracking, the camera would often unearth hidden elements or unveil shocking plot twists, thereby contributing to Hitchcock's suspenseful narrative.

The tracking shot, in particular, was a favorite tool of Hitchcock's. From the stunning overhead tracking shot in "The Birds" to the dramatic horizontal tracking shots in "Psycho", Hitchcock skillfully used this technique to build anticipation, introduce characters, or uncover vital plot points.

Another trademark Hitchcock technique was the effective use of bird's eye view shots. These high-angle shots often portrayed the characters from above, making them appear vulnerable and insignificant within their environment. This not only established an otherworldly perspective, but invoked feelings of fear and unease, craftily cementing the unnerving narratives Hitchcock is known for.

An unforgettable instance of Hitchcock's use of innovative camera angles was in "Vertigo", with its iconic 'Vertigo' shot, also known as a dolly zoom. By simultaneously zooming in and dollying out, or vice versa, Hitchcock immaculately captured the protagonist's acrophobia and disorientation to an extent that it made viewers feel they were losing their footing as well.

Even when there were no movements, a static camera had its own weighted and powerful implications in Hitchcock's tales. By letting the scene unfold without the interference of camera shakes or pans, he lets viewers form their own interpretation and be part of the storytelling process.

Hitchcock also proved a master at using camera placements to add depth to his stories. Often, his camera would peer from behind objects or characters, suggesting ele

ments of voyeurism, secrecy, or impending peril. This use of subjective camera effectively manages to draw the spectators in and generate shock and surprise.

The infamous shower scene in "Psycho", for instance, is an epitome of how the creative use of angles and positioning can add a sense of threat and anxiety. A high angle shot of the bathroom, through the translucent shower curtain, establishes both intimacy and apprehension. Here, the alternation between close-ups and extreme close-ups results in a thrilling spectacle of horror.

Similarly, Hitchcock also used low-angle shots for dramatic effect, often making characters appear intimidating or heroic. In "The Birds", Melanie's arrival at Bodega Bay shot from a low angle heralds not only her character's significance but also the looming disaster that her arrival invokes.

Dutch angles were another favorite tactic in Hitchcock's arsenal. By tilting the camera, he would create a disorienting and discomforting effect, implying psychological unrest or tension. Notably, in "Strangers on a Train", the skewed angles during the murder scene perfectly encapsulate the unnerving chaos and the protagonist's destabilization.

Above all, the camera served as Hitchcock's most dependable ally. It carried out his visions, expressed what words couldn't, and stealthily guided the viewers' emotions. The camera, in Hitchcock's deft hands, became a tool of suspense, an entity of storytelling, and an art form unto itself.

In the end, it's these extraordinary practices of camera angles and movements that make Hitchcock stand apart as a pioneer in the realm of narrative cinema. He used the camera as a director uses his cast - instructing, coercing, deceiving, all while pursuing a compelling story.

Whether you are an ardent cinephile or an amateur filmmaker, understanding and appreciating Hitchcock's utilization of camera movements and angles can give you fresh insights into his masterful storytelling. It opens up new horizons in the tantalizing realm of visual storytelling, strongly underlining how a camera's movement and angle can fundamentally alter a film's narrative.

Chapter 3: Iconic Techniques and Innovations

As our exploration into Hitchcock's craft continues, we delve into a few unique techniques that made him stand out among his contemporaries. The concept of the 'MacGuffin,' a term popularized by Hitchcock himself, signifies an object or element in the screenplay that propels the plot, despite not having any intrinsic importance to the story itself. This storytelling device is pivotal in many of Hitchcock's films, creating suspense and driving character actions. Hitchcock also innovated in his use of sound and music. Rather than merely being complementary, sound design in Hitchcock's films is integral to building tension, shaping the viewers' emotional response, and, at times, acting as an essential plot device. Noteworthy too is his masterful deployment of montage and editing techniques, an aspect of his filmic vocabulary that played a significant role in enhancing the impact and rhythm of his narratives. Hitchcock's non-traditional approach to editing, such as the use of 'cutting on action,' made his narratives intriguingly fluid and dynamic. Such techniques and innovations, revolutionary for their time, constitute an intrinsic part of the director's signature style, contributing to the enduring allure of his works.

The MacGuffin

In the realm of filmmaking, there are various devices and elements utilized to drive an engaging narrative forward. For Alfred Hitchcock, his choice narrative device was the "MacGuffin."

A term frequently used within the screenplay cycle, a MacGuffin is essentially an object, event, or character in a film that serves as the pivotal catalyst or focal point of the plot. It is an element that precipitates the course of action or the quest that characters undergo. However, a MacGuffin's appeal lies not so much in its intrinsic value or function, but in the importance that characters assign to it.

Generously used throughout Hitchcock's filmography, from "The 39 Steps" to "North by Northwest", the introduction of a MacGuffin would set the ball rolling, with the characters being propelled into a twisted web of events and circumstances. Despite this, the essential function—the MacGuffin served within the narrative—is often obscure or even irrelevant to the audience. In Hitchcock's hands, though, it morphs into a powerful tool that shapes the entire structure of the film.

One of the most definitive instances of a MacGuffin can be found in "Vertigo". In this cinematic masterpiece, an ostensibly possessed woman named Madeleine becomes the MacGuffin around which the spiraling narrative revolves. Her mystifying affliction lures the protagonist, Scottie, into the deadly vortex of obsession and terror.

Similarly, in "North by Northwest," the critical government secrets coveted by mysterious agents and pursued relentlessly by the protagonist, Roger Thornhill, act as the MacGuffin. The audience never learns what these secrets contain, but their importance is signified by the characters' frantic and perilous chase.

Hitchcock's use of the MacGuffin is ingenious in two influential ways. First, he uses it as a compelling smoke screen. As viewers, we're drawn into the plot by the intrigue surrounding these MacGuffins, consuming our attention and fostering a mounting sense of suspense and tension. These enigmatic elements are the driving force behind Hitchcock's renown as the "Master of Suspense".

Second, by using MacGuffins as a center stage, Hitchcock strategically deploys this tool to build complex, engaging characters in his narratives. By observing how these characters react to and interact with the MacGuffin, we gain profound insights into their personalities, motivations, and fears. Though the MacGuffin itself often recedes into the background or vanishes entirely by the story's end, its impact on the characters and their development is immeasurable.

Take, for instance, the titular statue in "The Maltese Falcon". Although the audience never sees the statue's interior contents—the legendary falcon—the artifact's existence and its impact on the characters make for a captivating narrative framework.

Interestingly, Hitchcock's MacGuffins were usually tangible objects — a key, a briefcase, a statue. However, in some films like "Psycho", the MacGuffin was something intangible - a sense of dread, a perception of insanity. Both forms, however, serve the same critical function of providing the narrative's backbone.

Another crucial aspect about the MacGuffin is that it often undergoes a transformation during the film. What begins as an object of great value or significance frequently diminishes in importance as the narrative unfolds. This allows Hitchcock to divert audience attention towards the characters and their relationships rather than the MacGuffin itself.

What makes Hitchcock's use of the MacGuffin so exceptional is his understanding of its negligible importance for the audience. Instead of elaborating on its details or resolution, Hitchcock leverages the suspense and intrigue that the MacGuffin brings about in its wake. In doing so, he manages to weave narratives that delve deep into the psychology of his characters, rather than being focused on a pedestrian chase after the elusive MacGuffin.

In conclusion, the MacGuffin, as used by Hitchcock, acts as a strategic narrative device that kick-starts the plot and unearths its nuances. While the MacGuffin may be central to the film's plot, Hitchcock never allows it to overshadow elements like character development or relationship dynamics. Through this seemingly simple narrative device, he created cinematic realms imbued with a lasting sense of suspense, mystery, and tension, forever shaping the tapestry of suspense and thriller genres.

Use of Sound and Music

The use of sound and music in Alfred Hitchcock's movies was an integral part of his storytelling. Hitchcock's mastery in the use of sound and music fully immersed audiences in his cinematic universe, heightening the emotional response and enhancing the narrative's momentum.

Sound in Hitchcock's films is not limited to mere background noise or "soundtrack." It is employed as a narrative tool in its own right. A classic example is the seagulls squawking or the children's screams in "The Birds." In scenes without dialogue, ambient noise often became a character itself, sharpening suspense and invoking a sense of dread.

Similarly, in "Rear Window," Hitchcock utilized the varied sounds from different apartments to emphasize the protagonist's voyeurism. He also employed silence strategically in order to make ambient noises more profound and unsettling.

As evident in many of Hitchcock's films, sound is often used to replace visuals, indirectly suggesting terror, creating an atmosphere ripe with tension. The iconic shower scene in "Psycho" is a perfect example, where the high pitched slashing noises etched an unforgettable mark on viewers' minds, a testament to Hitchcock's mastery over the auditory element.

Hitchcock also used sound as a repetitive motif, providing foreshadowing or highlighting specific narrative elements. In "North by Northwest," the recurring sound of an approaching airplane generates tension and imminent danger, escalating the sense of urgency and suspense.

Another innovative aspect of Hitchcock's approach to sound was the use of "subjective sound," where the audio reflects the psychological state of a character. This is exceptionally illustrated in "Vertigo," where eerie music mirrors the protagonist's fear and disorientation.

When it comes to music, Hitchcock collaborated with composer Bernard Herrmann on several notable films. Herrmann's genius matched Hitchcock's cinematography, with them together creating scores that not only heightened suspense but also contributed to the film's overall storytelling.

"Psycho" perhaps provides the most memorable score. Herrmann's innovative dissonant violin screeches in the shower scene not only remarkably enhance the shock and terror but is also frequently synonymous with murder or violence in pop culture.

In "Vertigo," Herrmann used a swirling harp and strings motif to represent the dizzying fear of heights, while in "North by Northwest," the pulsating, urgent score adds to the thrilling aspects of the chase.

The scores, composed by Herrmann for Hitchcock's films, were not meant just as accompaniments but became integral components of the viewing experience. They stand out, making a distinct contribution to the narrative's direction and character development.

Hitchcock's unique approach to sound and music undoubtedly extended his storytelling prowess, proving instrumental in establishing mood, enhancing suspense, and unsettling audience expectations.

In conclusion, the ingenious use of sound and music was an essential facet of Hitchcock's filmmaking process. Whether to increase tension, suggest threat, represent a character's mental state or make an indiscernible narrative element coherent, Hitchcock transcended the norms of his time, pioneering a precedent for future filmmakers to utilize these elements to their full capacity.

The atmospheric soundscapes and evocative musical scores in Hitchcock's greatest films are not mere extras but key storytellers and fixtures that affect how we interact with the narrative. They echo Hitchcock's creative bravura, his unmatched expertise to engage, captivate, and terrify, qualities that etch his masterpieces in global cinematic history.

Montage and Editing Techniques

The realm of Alfred Hitchcock's genius resides not just in his capacity show the story on screen, but also in his ability to shape, manipulate, and guide his narrative through his editing choices. The methods he developed not only resonated through his own work but revolutionized the ways filmmakers approached montage and editing techniques.

The term montage is a technique in film editing, involving a series of quick cuts to different images, often set to music, to express a passage of time, build up tension, or communicate an idea. Hitchcock achieved a degree of mastery over this technique and used it to establish a distinctive visual style.

In many of his films, Hitchcock utilized montage to build suspense and heighten dramatic situations without showcasing any explicit violence. The shower scene in "Psycho" is one such example. The montage of quick cuts heightens the intensity of the scene, making it more terrifying than the act itself. Here, Hitchcock employed montage to let viewers' imagination fill in the gaps, ultimately making the viewers themselves complicit in the creation of violence and horror they experience.

Another example of Hitchcock's use of montage appears in "The Birds" where a series of rapid shots from different angles convey the chaos caused by the attacking birds without showing much actual violence. The sequence of school children running from the attacking birds is a series of rapid cuts, where Hitchcock allows the terror to build sequentially, with each cut quickening the pace and raising the sense of panic.

Similarly, Hitchcock used editing techniques to demonstrate his characters' psychological states. In "Vertigo", a dolly zoom effect, sometimes known as 'The Vertigo Effect', was used to depict the protagonist's acrophobia. This innovative application of camera and editing techniques further exemplified Hitchcock's ability to create a sense of disorientation and dread within his audience by visualizing the psychological realities his characters were enduring.

Decades before the invention of the Steadicam, Hitchcock, with his movie "Rope," experimented with extremely long takes, connecting each take seamlessly through a careful use of mise-en-scène and editing. He aimed to create the illusion of watching events unfold in real-time to increase the tension and realism of the narrative.

In "North by Northwest", Hitchcock's editing shines in the famous crop duster scene. By using a series of short establishing shots and increasingly rapid cross-cutting between the protagonist and the approaching plane, the scene intensifies the sense of menace and inevitable danger. The intensity peaks with the plane's spectacular crash into a fuel tanker, a sequence realized through careful editing.

A unique feature of Hitchcock's editing technique was his use of point of view (POV) shots. Hitchcock often intercut between a character's reaction and what they are looking at in order to ramp up the tension. One of the best examples of this is in "Rear Window" where the entire story unfolds through the protagonist's point of view. Audiences are tightly bound to the lead character's viewpoint, giving them a sense of participation in the narrative.

One of Hitchcock's lesser-known films, "Strangers on a Train", highlights another editing technique known as parallel editing. The film cuts between two different events that are happening simultaneously, building suspense as the audience anticipates the two events converging.

Knowledge about the "Kuleshov Effect" - a film editing effect demonstrated by Soviet filmmaker Lev Kuleshov in the 1920s - greatly influenced Hitchcock's montage and editing techniques. Essentially, the Kuleshov Effect suggested that viewers derive more meaning from the interaction of two back-to-back shots than from a single shot in isolation. Beautifully adapted and developed by Hitchcock, this concept contributed significantly to the effectiveness of his films.

In his film "The Birds", Hitchcock utilized a combination of back projection and editing to create an effectively terrifying bird attack sequence. It is a fine demonstration of how montage and meticulous editing can be used to orchestrate a highly impactful scene that leaves a lasting impression.

The editing techniques employed by Hitchcock went beyond simple story construction. He used them to convey a specific mood, manipulate audience emotions, and thereby create a distinctive and unique viewer experience. The connection Hitchcock established between editing and storytelling was truly ahead of his time and continues to be influential in contemporary cinema.

Just as his narratives involved unexpected twists and turns, so too did Hitchcock's editing techniques. When coupled with his innovative storytelling, avant-garde techniques, and undeniable cinematic poise, it is no wonder that Alfred Hitchcock has left an indelible mark on the art of film editing and montage.

Looking beyond the suspense and thrill that Hitchcock is known for, it is his innovative editing and montage techniques that truly made him a master filmmaker. Through his films, he redefined standard conventions, always pushing the envelope of what might be expected, extending beyond the script to mingle with the viewer's mind.

Chapter 4: Analyzing "Psycho"

Delving into the depths of one of Hitchcock's most infamous thrillers, "Psycho" has become a staple of film studies worldwide. Its nail-biting plot delves into the macabre mind of the unforgettable character Norman Bates, mingling the terrifying and the taboo to create a narrative that still shocks audiences today. The film's chilling themes touch on mental instability, duality of personality, and mistaken identity, all embodied by the character residing at the sinister Bates Motel. Yet, it's the genius in how these themes are cinematically presented that truly cements Hitchcock's mastery. His purposeful framing and use of shadows craft an oppressive atmosphere, while the characteristic camera movements and angles give the audience a voyeuristic perspective that is innately uncomfortable. A striking example of Hitchcock's innovation is the infamous shower scene which, through rapid montage editing and painstaking attention to detail, has become one of the most recognizable scenes in cinematic history. The influence and impact of "Psycho" is broad in scope, echoing throughout the decades and standing as a testament to Hitchcock's abundant creativity. The resonance of such a brilliant film is evidence of its longevity, demonstrating the timeless power of storytelling and visual innovation.

Plot and Themes

Throughout Hitchcock's illustrious career, a meticulous focus on plot and themes emerged as a cornerstone of his storytelling style. In his groundbreaking production

"Psycho," this is quite clear. The plot maneuvers through unexpected twists and turns, immersing viewers in a riveting story centered on deceit, madness, and murder.

The initial narrative focuses on Marion Crane's desperate attempt to escape with stolen money, but a twist pulls the viewer into the realm of the infamous Bates Motel. Changing the protagonist mid-narrative, Hitchcock turns the viewer's attention to Norman Bates' peculiar relationship with his mother and his split personality disorder, two elements that would lay the groundwork for future psychological thrillers.

The overarching themes of "Psycho" revolve around duality and deception. While the seemingly harmless Norman hosts Marion prior to her murder, it's revealed he is not as innocent as he appears. Deception is further highlighted by the stolen money storyline, which eventually buries itself under the weight of the film's more gruesome narrative.

"Psycho" reminds viewers of their inner fears and uncovers the dark corners of an otherwise ordinary exterior. Duality, as epitomized by Bates' dual personality and the film's plot twists, reflects a recurring theme in Hitchcock's work. In the master's hands, the ordinary becomes menacing, creating a sense of suspense, doom, and panic.

Another Hitchcockian masterpiece, "Vertigo," displays the filmmaker's obsession with complex, intricate plots and recurring motifs. The story involves a retired detective suffering from acrophobia drawn into a puzzling case, only to fall in love with a woman who apparently does not exist.

The main theme of "Vertigo" is the destructive power of obsessive love. This is portrayed through Scottie's infatuation with Madeleine, and his subsequent obsession with Judy. Hitchcock brilliantly uses the metaphor of vertigo to depict Scottie's descent into madness and obsession.

A remarkable plot technique employed in "Vertigo" is the cyclical narrative. Two almost identical sequences occur, with the second reflecting the first but with a critical shift. In an eerie recurrence, Scottie encounters look-alike women, his emotions intertwined with déjà vu and the fear of confrontation with his past.

Moving on to "The Birds," Hitchcock adapts a somewhat straightforward narrative with unlikely elements to burrow deep into audience's primal fears. The prolonged shots of the birds slowly assembling and the mounting tension it builds before each attack is nothing short of a cinematic marvel.

The theme of chaos versus order is predominantly featured in "The Birds." The inexplicable bird attacks symbolize nature's revolt against humanity, a disorder shattering the serene facade of Bodega Bay. Hitchcock leaves the ending ambiguous, keeping audiences on edge even after the film ends, a testament to his magnificent filmmaking.

In "Rear Window," Hitchcock utilizes the confined setting to spin an intriguing tale about voyeurism, murder, and suspense. The apartment complex serves as a stage where various dramas unfold before Jeff's watchful gaze. Each window opens up another story, another life fraught with secrets and deceit. One of the critical themes in this film is the isolation within a community, further emphasized by the voyeuristic setting and plot.

"North by Northwest" melds tension and humor effortlessly, exploring themes of mistaken identities and a constant pursuit. Roger Thornhill's adventure, filled with dangerous scenarios and escapades, entangles him in a thrilling game of cat and mouse, while highlighting the theme of the facade versus reality, an element consistent with Hitchcock's oeuvre.

"Rope" and "Strangers on a Train," albeit lesser-known, delve into subjects like Nietzschean philosophy, the banality of evil, and psychological manipulation. These films use innovative techniques to tell dramatically different narratives, all while exploring themes of morality, guilt, and justice coated in suspense and thriller genre trappings.

One of the many reasons why Hitchcock's films have stood the test of time is his unmatched ability to weave in complex and dramatic themes within the framework of popular, accessible cinema. His gripping narratives and innovative storytelling techniques invite the audience not merely to watch but to partake in every twist and turn on the journey, leaving them mesmerized long after the curtain falls.

In concluding, Hitchcock's films, with their intricate plots and resonant themes, have played a vital role in forming the touchstone for cinematic suspense and psychological thrillers. From "Psycho" to "North by Northwest," his films embody a timeless, captivating artistry that continues to influence contemporary cinema, proving his indelible mark as the unrivaled Master of Suspense.

Cinematic Techniques

Let's turn our gaze to the cinematic techniques that Hitchcock masterfully employed. Hitchcock was hailed as a master manipulator of the medium of film, tirelessly honing these unique techniques to perfection over his distinguished career.

First and foremost, Hitchcock was a pioneer of what is now widely known as the 'point of view' (POV) shot. This technique placed viewers in the shoes of the character, making them participants in the narrative rather than mere observers. This sense of intimacy and immediacy amplified the emotions and suspense within Hitchcock's films and has become a staple of thriller and horror cinema.

Another recurring technique under Hitchcock's belt was the use of the subjective camera. Here, the audience sees exactly what the character sees, creating deep emotional bonds. Such camera work was expertly employed in "Rear Window". In a way, the viewers become accomplices, trapped in the protagonist's voyeuristic fascination.

Hitchcock was also celebrated for his innovative use of the 'dolly zoom', a cinematic technique commonly referred to as the 'Vertigo' effect. This technique creates a jarring visual effect that combines a dolly in with a zoom out, or vice versa. By manipulating focal length and camera distance, Hitchcock was able to create a feeling of disorientation and unease, reflecting the protagonist's fear and instability in the film "Vertigo".

A unique element that Hitchcock rarely abandoned was his meticulous approach to color. Whether it was the vibrant, yet eerie hues in one of his most vibrant films like "The Birds", or the monochrome palette used in "Psycho", color was an impactful tool in his storytelling process, establishing mood, and highlighting important narrative details.

The master of suspense also knew the power of a well-placed silhouette. Sharp, dark outlines against a stark background added texture to the characters, and tension to the narrative. In "Psycho", the silhouette of Norman Bates' mother in the window is a haunting image viewers cannot easily forget.

In creating suspense and terror, Hitchcock smartly used high-angle shots. These shots were crucial to his storytelling, as they positioned the audience to look down from a high angle, making characters seem vulnerable or insignificant, often indicating a change in power dynamics.

Low-angle shots, on the other hand, were used to amplify a sense of dominance or looming threat. We see this in the infamous crop duster scene in "North by Northwest", where the plane looms menacingly large in the sky, suggesting the deadly threat it poses.

In tandem with these high-angle and low-angle shots, Hitchcock committed to the use of the 'dutch tilt', a camera technique that involves tilting the camera on its axis to create an unsettling, disoriented feeling, indicative of psychological unease or tension within the character.

Hitchcock also demonstrated a mastery of symbolism in his films, a technique often interlinked with his use of so-called 'MacGuffins'; objects or goals that they characters pursue, serving as catalysts for the plot. In "North by Northwest", the sought-after microfilm is a moot point; in "Rope", the real focus isn't the murdered person but the murderers' perverse curiosity.

The placement of characters within a frame was another of Hitchcock's unique techniques. He often manipulated the physical position and perspective of characters to emphasize their psychological state. The character blocking in "Vertigo", for instance, explores the relationship between Scottie and Madeleine in physical terms, using proximity, positioning, and symmetry.

Lastly, Hitchcock's intricate approach to sound design cannot be left unnoticed. He championed the idea that sound and silence could be just as impactful, if not more, than visual stimuli for invoking tension or suspense.

Hitchcock fiercely believed in the power of 'pure cinema', a form of storytelling that relied primarily on visuals. The shower scene from "Psycho", for instance, is a masterful exercise in pure cinema, as it uses visual cues and sound to create a sense of terror and brutality, without the viewer ever witnessing the actual act of violence.

In essence, Hitchcock's brilliant use of these cinematic techniques transformed the entire landscape of suspense and thriller cinema. His approach to POV shots, subjective camera, color design, high-angle and low-angle shots, camera tilting, and sound design were all revolutionary at their time and have had lasting resonance within modern cinema.

Documenting all the techniques Hitchcock employed and discussing their intricacies would require an entirely separate volume. However, understanding the ones mentioned is a good starting point towards appreciating the genius of Alfred Hitchcock, and the profound impact he had on the cinematic world.

Influence and Impact

The influence and impact of Alfred Hitchcock's "Psycho" permeate not only the world of cinema but also popular culture, becoming a reference point for future generations of filmmakers. It's undeniable that the ingenious techniques especially the cinematography adopted by Hitchcock to create a spine-chilling suspense in the film changed the landscape of thriller movies forever.

Take, for example, the shower scene that lasts only a few minutes but has been discussed and dissected for decades.

The film often referred to as the 'mother of the modern horror genre,' took the medium of storytelling in cinema to unexplored heights. And much of that storytelling capability comes directly from the film's cinematography.

Hitchcock once said, "The better the villain, the better the film." In "Psycho," we see this statement come to life in the unforgettable performance of Anthony Perkins as Norman Bates. This performance and the development of the character Bates, along with the innovative cinematic techniques, have profoundly influenced several films, from "The Texas Chainsaw Massacre" to "Silence of the Lambs" and beyond.

The cinematic techniques employed by Hitchcock in "Psycho," such as unique camera angles, close-ups, and strategic use of light and shadow, have inspired filmmakers globally. From the suspenseful horror movies of the late 20th century to the modern horror/mystery films of today, the impact of Hitchcock's style of storytelling is evident.

Hitchcock's use of the camera was revolutionary in defining the genre of suspense and horror. By employing a range of cinematographic techniques from unexpected camera movements to skewed angles, he was able to physically unsettle viewers and manipulate their expectations. This approach to visual storytelling inspired a new generation of filmmaking that continues to evolve today.

His use of sound, silence, and music further elevated this genre. The screeching violins during the iconic shower scene in "Psycho" created an insurmountable sense of fear. It showcased how sound and music could be integral to the storytelling process and not just documentative. This innovative use of sound technology is evident in today's suspense and horror movies.

When discussing the influence of Hitchcock, it's impossible to ignore his decision to shock the viewers by eliminating the leading lady at the start of "Psycho". This was an unprecedented move at the time and helped make the film unpredictable and suspenseful. This storytelling twist became a new narrative path for modern cinema to explore, paving the way for unexpected character exits and unconventional plot developments.

Additionally, Hitchcock's ability to create personal tension through his characters was a critical factor driving the audience's interest. The most iconic depiction of this is the development of Norman Bates in "Psycho". The character's complexities and mannerisms, charted meticulously by Hitchcock, prompted filmmakers to take a more in-depth look at their characters, moving beyond simple good versus evil dichotomies.

The impact of Alfred Hitchcock's narrative style, use of imagery, and character development extends to television. From "Twin Peaks" to "Bates Motel," Hitchcock's influence bridges the gap between film and television, proving that his techniques are viable across multiple media types.

The influence of "Psycho" transcends cinema, infiltrating the worlds of literature, music, and visual art. The iconic imagery Hitchcock created in the film has been replicated and referenced in countless mediums, reinforcing the cultural significance of his work.

Hitchcock's manipulation of viewers' expectations has fundamentally changed audience perceptions of what a film could and should do, making him a beacon within the film industry. Each subsequent generation of filmmakers examines his work for a deeper understanding of visual storytelling's intricacies and potential.

Overall, the impact of "Psycho" and by extension, Hitchcock's work, was far-reaching. It changed how viewers perceived cinema and how filmmakers approached storytelling. There is no denying that many elements present in modern suspense and horror films can be traced back to Hitchcock's originality, creativity, and unique interpretative vision.

Thus, regardless of the evolution of technology and the transformation of film over time, Hitchcock's legacy remains intact. His influence and impact continue to be thoroughly studied, admired and emulated by film enthusiasts, film students, and filmmakers around the world.

In conclusion, Alfred Hitchcock's imaginative approach to creating "Psycho" revolutionized cinema. His understanding of character development, his mastery of suspenseful storytelling, his innovative use of cinematography elements have all had a profound impact on film history. There is much to be learned from studying his body of work, a learning that transcends theory and touches upon the intangible aspects of intuition, creativity, and the human psychological interplay that Hitchcock portrayed so masterfully in his film, "Psycho".

Chapter 5: A Closer Look at "Vertigo"

Turning our attention to Hitchcock's spellbinding representation of obsession and identity in "Vertigo," we delve into the weave of artful narrative and transformative cinematography that elevated the movie into its classic status. The movie's plot is spun around a fascinating swirl of psychological manipulation and spiraling fear that keeps the audience on the edge of their seat. The techniques employed in the film are nothing short of groundbreaking, with each scene meticulously crafted to depict the protagonist's disoriented state of mind. Hitchcock's fondness for long-shots, unconventional camera angles, and expert framing are especially evident in "Vertigo," as they work together to underline Scottie's vertiginous affliction. Meanwhile, the use of color and light fully exploit the emotional depth of the unfolding drama. In particular, the startlingly innovative 'Vertigo effect'—where the camera moves backward while zooming in—remarkably illustrated the unsettling feeling of acrophobia. Ultimately, it was this extraordinary blend of visual artistry, superbly nuanced characters, a riveting storyline, and Hitchcock's masterful direction that harmonized into the making of this unforgettable classic.

Story Analysis

At the heart of every Alfred Hitchcock film is a meticulously crafted, layered narrative. A closer analysis of the story structure in "Vertigo" provides a unique window into Hitchcock's filmmaking genius.

"Vertigo" starts as a detective story. Its protagonist, Scottie, is a retired San Francisco detective with a fear of heights. He is hired by an old friend to investigate his wife, Madeleine, who the friend believes is possessed. It's a fairly straightforward detective narrative, but it's here where Hitchcock begins to layer the complexity.

The sense of the uncanny is disrupted when Scottie falls for Madeleine, and after her apparent death, his feelings spiral into obsession. What started off as a straightforward detective story morphs into a tale of dark obsession, blurring the line between reality and fantasy. This twist in the narrative is evidence of Hitchcock's unique storytelling approach, leading the audience along one path, only to suddenly shift to another.

This technique throws off audience expectations, creating a lingering sense of unease. Hitchcock doesn't just want to entertain his audience, he wants to unsettle them. In "Vertigo," the unexpected story twists leave the viewer disoriented, mimicking Scottie's own feelings of vertigo.

A deep dive into the character of Scottie also provides insights into his creator's narrative techniques. Scottie is a flawed character; his unreliability is revealed in his actions and decisions. By the film's conclusion, the audience realizes they have been viewing events through a biased lens.

Examining another aspect of "Vertigo," one also finds in its story a meditation on identity and illusion. The characters of Madeleine and Judy represent competing identities; Madeleine, an obsessed-upon specter, and Judy, the real woman behind the fabrication. Their existence becomes a haunting exploration of illusion and reality.

This concept of double identity becomes a repeated motif in Hitchcock's later works, demonstrating his ongoing exploration of similar themes. From Madeleine and Judy, to Marion and Norman in "Psycho," or Roger and Kaplan in "North by Northwest," Hitchcock frequently toys with dual identities to disconcert the audience and subvert narrative norms.

The story also cleverly reuses elements from Hitchcock's past films. For instance, Madeleine's obsessive investigation into a tragic historical figure parallels the detective stories in Hitchcock's early British thrillers. By revisiting earlier themes and intertwining them in fresh, innovative narratives, Hitchcock showcased his ability to innovate within his own established genre.

"Vertigo's" plot also pays homage to the silent era of film. A significant portion of the story is told visually, with minimal dialogue. This silent storytelling emphasizes the symbolic and visual power of film, techniques Hitchcock learned in the silent film era.

Moreover, Hitchcock subverts the romantic conventions of mid-20th-century cinema. Love stories of that era often featured a heroic man saving a damsel in distress. But in "Vertigo," the man not only fails to save the woman he loves, but he also drives her to destruction out of his own obsession. This subversion illustrates Hitchcock's willingness to challenge the status quo, often in dark and unsettling ways.

Scottie's desperation to recreate Madeleine illustrates another critical theme: the danger of living in the past. This narrative element resonates with post-war audiences attempting to reconcile significant cultural changes and a longing for the simplicity of former times.

To conclude, the "Vertigo" story analysis highlights Hitchcock's ability to construct complex, layered narratives that subvert audience expectations. By dissecting his characters, motifs, thematic elements, and plot structure, we uncover a narrative style inextricably linked to Hitchcock's identity as a filmmaker. A nuanced understanding of his unique story construction deepens the viewers' appreciation of his cinema as they continue their exploration endeavors through his filmography.

Therefore, story analysis allows us to better understand and appreciate Hitchcock's films on a deeper level. It's a lens into his exceptional narrative techniques, thematic preoccupations, and filmmaking genius; leaving an indelible influence on cinema that continues to the present day.

Visual Elements

Alfred Hitchcock's films are a testament to his keen understanding of the visual elements of cinema. He was arguably one of the first directors to truly understand and utilize the power of the visual to evoke emotions and drive narratives. This chapter will delve into a deeper look into his use of imagery, using "Vertigo" - the film that is perhaps the greatest display of his visual finesse - as primary examples.

Hitchcock's use of color in "Vertigo" is masterful. The film's palette is dominated by a range of blues, which weaves a mood of melancholy, confusion, and suspense, directly reflecting the state of the film's central character, John 'Scottie' Ferguson. In contrast, scenes featuring Madeleine are mostly painted in vivid and warm colors, providing a stark juxtaposition that enhances the storyline's tension.

Hitchcock's use of landscape in constructing his scenes is another important visual aspect. The cityscape of San

Francisco, with its dizzily sloping streets, towering buildings, and vast bay, provide a fitting backdrop for the story's themes of obsession, elevation, and vertigo. The relentless outlines of the city symbolize Scottie's mental state, ever-present and looming.

Hitchcock was often unconventional in his use of camera angles. In "Vertigo," he famously used an in-camera effect called a dolly zoom to depict the sensation of vertigo. This technique involves moving the camera away from a subject while simultaneously zooming in, creating a distorted perspective that intensifies a sense of disorientation and unease.

Apart from the camera angles, the manipulation of time and space through editing was another powerful visual tool in Hitchcock's cinematic repertoire. He often used cross-cutting to heighten the suspense, displaying two events occurring simultaneously to build up tension. Moreover, Hitchcock frequently employed flashbacks, not merely as narrative devices, but as a way to visually represent a character's psychological state.

Hitchcock's visual storytelling was not only restricted to the overt, but his use of hidden visual cues also demonstrated his commitment to the visual form. For instance, flowers are prevalent in many scenes of "Vertigo." They subtly mirror Madeleine's transformation and indicate Scottie's encroaching obsession.

"Vertigo" is perhaps Hitchcock's most stylized film. Here, he experimented with many innovative techniques. Hitchcock toyed with color filters to give many scenes a dreamlike quality, accentuating the story's theme of illusion versus reality. The use of slow dissolving sequences created a hypnotic effect, helping to intensify the narrative's sense of unease and disorientation.

Another remarkable visual element is Hitchcock's use of shadows. The characters' dark silhouettes often communicate their emotions, hidden desires, or unspoken intents. To Hitchcock, the shadows can harbor deeper truths even than what is cast under the light.

A striking example of this is when Scottie pursues Madeleine to the Golden Gate Bridge. The director used the real location to great effect to cast gigantic shadows of the characters, amplifying their inner turmoil and enhancing the mystery surrounding Madeleine.

Costumes and props also play an integral role as visual elements in Hitchcock's films. In "Vertigo," the clothes worn by the characters are an integral part of the narrative. Madeleine's grey suit becomes an aura of enigma and obsession for Scottie. Judy's transformation into Madeleine, signaled largely by her donning the iconic grey suit, serve not only as plot devices, but encapsulate several themes of the movie within the visual realm.

Hitchcock's visual composition of frames was often meticulous, full of symmetries, and loaded with significance —a testament to his background in art direction and his sharp visual acumen. The study of the visual composition of his frames is an endeavor in understanding his unique storytelling style. An obsession with what is seen and unseen, marital infidelity, voyeurism; these themes become alive through his composition within the camera frame.

Visual motifs are recurring elements in 'Vertigo,' like spirals, mirrors, and portraits, each serving to remind us of the themes of deception, duality, obsession, and fear of heights.

The spiral motif is particularly significant, given its recurring appearance in the film's opening credits, Scottie's nightmare sequence, the staircase at the bell tower, and Madeleine's hairdo.

The portrait of Carlotta Valdes, a visual hint for Madeleine's supposed possession, is a key component of the mystery. Hitchcock uses the portrait tremendously to blur the line between reality and illusion, driving the narrative forward and dramatizing Scottie's obsession with Madeleine's likeness in it.

Hitchcock's clever and thoughtful use of mirrors further emphasizes the themes of duality and deception. Many scenes in 'Vertigo' feature characters mirrored or doubled, a constant reminder of the deceptive duplicity at play.

Whether through the use of color, camera angles, or visual cues, Hitchcock's mastery of the visual medium remains unparalleled. This chapter has examined how the master used visual elements to create suspense and tension, develop characters, and tell stories in ways that captivate and thrill audiences. From his strategic use of imagery to his innovative camera techniques, Hitchcock's unique visual style formed an essential component of his cinematic genius.

The Making of a Classic

When one thinks about Alfred Hitchcock's genius and how he reinvented cinema, their minds may naturally gravitate towards "Vertigo." This film demonstrated what we now refer to as quintessential Hitchcock: intriguing storytelling combined with incredibly precise visual composition. The making of the film was a journey of discovery, experimentation and the masterful use of elements of suspense, which ultimately pushed the boundaries of what was traditionally accepted in cinema.

Hitchcock's fascination with the inner workings of the human mind played a significant role in the development of "Vertigo." His quest for absolute control over his audience's emotions was accomplished through a plot full of misdirection, coupled with the ethereal visual elements set against the backdrop of a mesmerizingly haunting musical score.

The process began with a strong story. The plot of "Vertigo" was adopted from the novel 'D'entre les morts' (From Among the Dead) by Pierre Boileau and Thomas Narcejac. It explored themes of obsession, guilt, and identity that blended well into Hitchcock's narrative style. However, adaptation in itself was not enough; Hitchcock needed more. He added layers of complexity in the motives and psychologies of his characters, thereby turning a simple thriller into a psychological masterpiece.

Every scene in "Vertigo" is a masterpiece of cinematic craftsmanship. Hitchcock used a combination of meticulous set design and purposeful camera angles to maintain a mood of constant uneasiness. He consulted with his cinematographer, Robert Burks, and production designer, Henry Bumstead, to achieve his vision. The pair's use of color and the construction of elaborate sets allowed Hitchcock to create an atmosphere that went beyond the script.

One of the main elements that set "Vertigo" apart was the pioneering use of the dolly zoom, a camera technique that creates a disorienting, vertiginous effect. This was used to significant effect during the bell tower scene, adding to the protagonist's vertigo and general confusion, thus allowing the audience to empathize with his disorientation.

Also of note is Hitchcock's use of mirrors and reflections throughout the film, adding another level of complexity. Often, characters are shown in mirrors, simultaneously reflecting their physical presence and inner turmoil. This technique symbolized duality, identity, and perception, creating a sense of eeriness and continued suspense throughout the film.

The costuming in "Vertigo" was also a critical element in telling the layered story. Edith Head, Hitchcock's regular costume designer, created looks that emphasized each character's personality and state of mind. For instance, the transformation of Judy into Madeleine is strongly marked by changes in dress, hairstyle, and makeup, integral to the whole illusion of the plot.

The final piece of a successful Hitchcock film lies in the soundtrack. For "Vertigo", Hitchcock teamed up with Bernard Herrmann, resulting in an extremely powerful marriage between sound and image. The main theme provided an eerie, surreal quality, enhancing the sense of unease in the audience. The rhythm of the score mirrors Scottie's emotional state, increasing in intensity as his psychological condition worsens.

Despite its superb craftsmanship, though, "Vertigo" did not receive universal acclaim upon its release. Critics criticized the plot as overly complex, the runtime too long, and the pace quite slow. Yet, given time and much reflection, "Vertigo" slowly ascended to its rightful place as one of cinema's most extraordinary feats.

Its iconic imagery, groundbreaking techniques, and haunting themes have been influential to countless filmmakers. The film's eloquent exploration of voyeurism, identity, and disturbed psychological states has increasingly resonated with audiences over the years.

The film's journey was not a straight path to stardom but a slow climb - much like Scottie's climb up the mission tower. Just as Scottie has to overcome his physical vertigo, "Vertigo" needed to transcend original perception and critique to secure its place within cinematic history.

Looking back on the making of "Vertigo," it's clear that Hitchcock was not simply focused on creating a commercial thriller but a timeless piece of art. His commitment to pushing cinematic boundaries resulted in a haunting film that continues to challenge, inspire, and fascinate audiences over sixty years later.

In conclusion, the making of "Vertigo" is a testament to the genius of Alfred Hitchcock, a director unafraid to challenge the status quo. By seamlessly melding psychological distress with classic mystery, he transformed a simple narrative into a sensory experience that keeps audiences coming back, time and time again. The processes and techniques used in "Vertigo" are emblematic of Hitchcock's unique style, a style that continues to shape the cinematic landscape to this day.

Chapter 5: "The Birds" and the Power of Imagery

In a further exploration of Hitchcock's knack for crafting distinct cinema, we engross ourselves in "The Birds," a film prodigiously rooted in the power of imagery. We see a prevalence of symbolism and metaphor throughout this tale of nature's inexplicable revolt against mankind. Hitchcock knits this strange occurrence together by employing strong visual cues, inculcating the memorable sight of the birds themselves, which morph from incidental parts of the scenery into lethal antagonists. The film's stark contrasts between auditory aspects, jumping from unsettling silence to chaotic cacophonies of flapping wings and avian attacks, play a critical role in enriching the ominous atmosphere. While the special effects utilized may appear rudimentary by current standards, their execution was remarkably pioneering during its heyday. The meticulous arrangement of live and mechanic birds generated an uncanny blend of fear and fascination, attesting to Hitchcock's continuous ambition to push the boundaries of storytelling through visual and auditory enhancements. As we delve deeper, we recognize how "The Birds" has left an enduring legacy, not only within Hitchcock's catalog but also influencing future endeavors in the horror and thriller genres. Though the birds may not symbolize anything concrete, they're ever-powerful images that hint at universal fears, leading us to reflect on Mother Nature's wrath, and how sometimes, the most terrifying realities are the ones we can't comprehend.

Symbolism and Metaphor

One of the most distinctive aspects of Hitchcock's films is his use of symbolism and metaphor. These elements, often woven seamlessly into the fabric of his narratives, deepen the viewer's understanding of the plot and themes, often conveying information and meaning that can't be expressed through dialogue or action alone.

Take, for instance, Hitchcock's extensive use of birds as a symbol in "The Birds." Aside from the obvious fact that the birds, literally, embody the horror and chaos in the film, their presence also serves a metaphorical function that reflects on the film's critique of human nature. Birds usually symbolize freedom, but in this film, they're turned into malevolent beings that mirror the destructive tendencies of humans, providing a unique commentary on our simple assumptions about nature and the world we inhabit.

Hitchcock's use of symbolism extends beyond just recurring physical objects. He frequently utilized colors, sounds, and even character ticks or obsessions to further his storylines and plot. For instance, in "Vertigo," Madeleine's (played by Kim Novak) green dress and the red hues in Judy's (also Kim Novak) apartment add to the movie's surreal and somber tone.

In the same film, we find that the spiral, a symbolic figure representing vertigo and obsession, infuses the narrative structure. The symbolic spiral is seen not only in the architecture like the mission tower or staircase but also in Madeleine's hairstyle, adding a mesmerizing allure to her character.

The titular 'Rear Window' in Hitchcock's film of the same name is yet another example of metaphor. The window serves both as a literal window to 'real-life drama' unfolding in front of Jeff (James Stewart) and a symbolic window into the voyeurism ingrained in human nature.

Hitchcock's strategic use of mirrors in his films is another example of his symbolic genius. They frequently symbolize duality or the darker side of characters. This device is beautifully exercised in 'Psycho' where Marion Crane's reflection is shown in a mirror before her death, alluding to her impending doom.

Yet, Hitchcock's creativity doesn't stop at these physical and visual metaphors. He's also known for his groundbreaking audio symbolism. The unbearable shrieking of the violins in the shower scene of 'Psycho' will forever symbolize the terror of unexpected violence for audiences around the world.

Iconic as those high-pitched strings may be, this isn't the only time Hitchcock has used sound as an instrument of symbolism. In "The Birds," the initially peaceful twittering of birds slowly transforms into something malignant, mirroring the escalating horror in the plot.

Even the title of his films often adds an extra layer of metaphor and meaning. For instance, 'North by Northwest' is not a legitimate compass direction. The title suggests disorientation which brilliantly complements Roger Thornhill's (Cary Grant) plight in the film as he is tossed around by a case of mistaken identity.

Hitchcock also prominently used character obsessions and actions as symbolic devices to delineate and dissect their complex emotional and mental states. This is best portrayed in "Marnie," where the title character's compulsive thieving and lying symbolize her struggle with her tormented past.

It must be reiterated that these symbols and metaphors are never tacked on as afterthoughts in Hitchcock's films. Instead, they are woven meticulously into character undertones, cinematographic choices, and plot development, aligning perfectly with Hitchcock's intent to let the audience engage in a form of 'participatory viewing'.

In conclusion, the brilliance of Hitchcock's symbolism and metaphors lies in their subtlety. They don't flag down the audience's attention but lurk beneath the surface of the narrative, appearing more like an organic part of the story rather than an imposed symbolic device. This chapter elucidates how Hitchcock's visual and verbal metaphors enhance his storylines, adding depth and dimension to his masterful framework, revealing yet another layer of his cinematic genius.

Sound and Silence

The genius of Alfred Hitchcock reverberates through every scene and note of his films, but perhaps nowhere is his deftness more apparent than in his manipulation of soundscape and silence. His innovative use of these elements conjured an immersive atmosphere that became his signature and a masterclass for the future of filmmaking. In "The Birds," these elements are temperately entwined to heighten suspense and imprint lasting impressions.

Hitchcock used sound techniques to its fullest extent as a narrator of his stories. He understood the aural sphere's potential to elicit emotions, command attention, and suggest the unseen. In "The Birds," nature's cacophony becomes a sinister entity, its roiling crescendo signaling the imminent danger more potent than any dialogue could convey. The screeching and cawing of the birds are manipulated to create a discordant symphony that intensifies the terror, demonstrating the director's craft at drawing upon the soundscape to create a foreboding atmosphere.

Conversely, Hitchcock's use of silence was equally powerful. He was aware that absence of sound could induce a sense of unease and anticipation. Moments of silence in his films were often precursors to suspenseful scenes. The absence of a musical score in "The Birds" highlighted the alarming sounds of the avian onslaught and amplified the suspense and tension. The quietude was as piercing as the relentless cacophony of the birds, and the blend of the two created an audio experience that bespoke imminent danger and filled viewers with dread.

Moreover, Hitchcock's brilliant use of diegetic sound, a sound that naturally takes place within the world of the film, morphs into a formidable character in "The Birds". The wingbeats, squawks, and screams tell a story, dictating the pace and flow of the story, even replacing traditional dialogues. And yet, these sounds are organic and intrinsic to the narrative, unlike an orchestral score overlaid onto a film. It is the orchestration of these natural sounds that creates the ambiance of the film, driving the suspense forward.

The absence of non-diegetic music in "The Birds" was a calculated risk. Hitchcock was bucking the Hollywood norm of heavily orchestrated films. Instead, Hitchcock's eerie silence filled the viewers' senses with dread and uncertainty. His bet paid off, demonstrating his understanding of sound's power—or its absence—to evoke fear and suspense, and his ability to manipulate it masterfully.

It's worth noting Hitchcock's innovative use of technological advancements in sound engineering during "The Birds" filming. Sound designers were tasked with creating bird noises that were terrifying yet realistic, which was a considerable challenge. Special sound devices were crafted to mix various bird sounds and alter their intonations to create the terrifying cacophony heard in the film. This technical savvy enhanced the overall film experience.

A snapshot of Hitchcock's ingenious sound structuring occurs in the scene where Tippi Hedren's character, Melanie Daniels, walks up to the school. As she sits on a bench smoking a cigarette, a flock of crows silently gathers on the playground behind her. It is only when she notices the birds does the terrifying reality sets in. Hitchcock intentionally decreased the ambient sounds during this scene to build suspense. The following sudden explosive burst of bird sounds then accelerates the tension to an incredible degree.

Albeit less apparent, the manipulation of sound extends to human voices. In this film, screams were meticulously crafted, many times running overture of the raucous birds to heighten the terror. Hitchcock modifies the volume, tone, and timing of screams with a composer's precision, using them as an auditory symbol of terror.

An intimate understanding of the audience's psyche was behind this effective orchestration of sound. Cognizant of sound's impression on the subconscious, Hitchcock used sound and silence to play on primal fears, giving viewers an immersive, palpable fear that lingered long after the film ended. This aspect made his films unforgettable and demonstrated his innovative approach to filmmaking.

The genius of sound and silence in "The Birds" and other Hitchcock's films cannot be overlooked. They were significant elements in his suspense-building toolkit, not merely background noise or random sound effects. This understanding of audio engineering was far ahead of its time and remains a study of interest in contemporary filmmaking.

Alfred Hitchcock's artistry breathed life into the silent and unconventional elements, vividly painting his narrative in audio visuals that gripped viewers and rattled their nerves. His use of soundscape and punctuating silence allows the viewer to engage on a more visceral level by tapping into their subconscious fears. It is this genius combination of sound and silence that made Hitchcock's suspenseful scenes unforgettable.

Every sweep of wings, menacing squawk of crows, screams, and the crawling silence in "The Birds" was Hitchcock's deliberate arrangement. From chaos to calm, he intricately wove silence and sound, using them as omnipotent characters to dominate his infamous suspense scenes, serving as a testament to his genius that continues to resonate in the annals of film history.

Visual Effects and Legacy

In "The Birds", Alfred Hitchcock's innovative use of visual effects paved the way for future film techniques, leaving a reverberant legacy in the realm of cinema. With the utmost attention to detail, Hitchcock crafted intense visuals, which were powerful enough to invoke explicit terror and yet subtle enough to suggest the psychological dimension of fear.

The visual effects of "The Birds" were groundbreaking for their era; the blend of live-action and mechanical birds, combined with innovative special effects, resulted in unforgettable scenes of horror. The birds in the film, real or not, were manipulated through a blend of careful framing, forced perspective, and notions of movement, cleverly devised to adopt a menacing aspect rarely attributed to such common creatures.

The scenes involving bird attacks were particularly notable. Their execution and resulting depiction featured a mix of live and mechanical birds masterfully edited to heighten authenticity. The trick was to focus the audience's attention on the chaos of these scenes, blurring the line between artificial and real.

Absence of explicit gore and reliance on viewer's imagination was a ripe challenge for Hitchcock. Overcoming this through innovative visual effects was a significant accomplishment. Using an optically printed process known as the sodium vapor process or yellow screen, Hitchcock was able to superimpose the birds convincingly into scenes, striking a fine balance between horror and believability.

One pivotal scene that speaks volumes of Hitchcock's visual mastery is the famous playground scene. Tippi Hedren's character, Melanie Daniels, sits oblivious while crows accumulate on the playground behind her. The scene builds from a placid afternoon to a subtle menace using effective visual cues without the need for dialogue.

"The Birds" also introduced a unique visual effect: the high-speed reverse zoom, popularly known as the 'dolly zoom' or 'Vertigo shot.' This technique would later be embraced by the film industry and is seen in various films, thus etching Hitchcock's influence into the fabric of cinema.

"The Birds" remains remarkably fresh in its impact and aesthetic despite the technological advances seen in later years. This is largely due to Hitchcock's expertise in weaving a physical reality with psychological terror – a blend that, when mastered, remains impervious to obsolescence.

From a modern perspective, the combination of practical effects and pioneering visual effects also offered a matte painting projection technique that allowed for an increased level of believability. Today, these visual effects techniques may seem dated, yet they paved the way for the advent of more advanced technologies in modern cinema.

The influence of "The Birds" on contemporary movies and filmmakers is undeniable. Many directors, including modern masters of suspense such as M. Night Shyamalan, cite the movie as a major influence. Its techniques have been emulated and built upon by legions of filmmakers eager to capture Hitchcock's expert blend of tension and terror.

Apart from its technical achievements, the thematic richness and behavioral precision of "The Birds" have ensured its standing as a cornerstone Hitchcock film. The range of human fears and foibles it projects—a mother's over-protection, a lover's jealousy, our collective denial of ecological balance—remain strikingly relevant today, thus expanding the film's legacy.

Novel and ambitious in each frame with an unwavering focus on visual storytelling, "The Birds" was a cinematic milestone. In an age where CGI dominates the big screen, the film's practical effects and clever application of optical illusions underscore a dynamic approach towards visual storytelling.

"The Birds" left a profound impact not only on the viewers but also on the entire horror genre. From its specific editing techniques to its innovative use of sound design, "The Birds" has left an indelible mark on contemporary filmmaking by setting new standards for suspense and terror.

As with any great and innovative artist, Hitchcock's work on "The Birds" changed the course of his industry, making him a true pioneer in visual effects. His legacy is not only a body of extraordinary work but also a roadmap for future generations to push the boundaries of what is possible in cinematic storytelling.

Thus, the visual effects in "The Birds", though produced with the relatively limited technology of the time, have had a profound and lasting impact on the art of film. The influence of Alfred Hitchcock and "The Birds" continues to reverberate through decades, consistently reminding us that a filmmaker's only constraint is the expanse of their own imagination.

Chapter 7: "Rear Window" and the Voyeuristic Lens

In the realm of cinematic mastery, "Rear Window" stands as a stellar testament to Hitchcock's use of voyeurism as a narrative technique. We're invited into the world of L.B. "Jeff" Jefferies, a professional photographer confined to a wheelchair in his small apartment. The cinematographic treatment of this physical limitation gives birth to a fascinating exploration of voyeurism. We, like Jeff, look out onto a world restricted to the view of his rear window. Every frame in this film becomes a 'window' into the lives of the various characters, revealing their quirks, dramas, and secrets. It's a looking glass into the human condition, with Hitchcock exploiting the audience's proclivity for voyeurism in order to heighten the suspense. The cinematography employed in the film gives a new dimension to this voyeuristic perspective with meticulous framing and focused camera movements. Each shot is designed for us to peek into the lives of these characters, making us complicit voyeurs. In doing so, Hitchcock not only creates a thrilling narrative with cultural relevance, but also gives us a study in the ethical implications of voyeurism, a motif that continues to resonate in contemporary cinema.

Themes and Motifs

Alfred Hitchcock was a master of suspense and fear, melding visual aesthetics to enhance a story's psychological depth. Integral to this pursuit was his use of recurring motifs and themes. These symbols, whether objects or subliminal mirroring of human behaviors, helped weave intricate narratives that still captivate audiences today.

A recurring motif in Hitchcock's films is the 'blonde heroine.' These female characters, often icy, sophisticated, and elegant, are integral to his films. They exhibit a complex blend of vulnerability and resilience, embodied by actresses such as Grace Kelly, Kim Novak, and Tippi Hedren. This motif goes far beyond mere physical appearance, as it explores societal perceptions, sexual politics and vulnerability.

Hitchcock often painted a grim picture of romantic relationships. Forms of deceit, betrayal, manipulation, and suspicion often plagued his characters, adding to the underlying threat in their ordinary lives. These conflicts did not just fuel the narrative tension; they also amplified the psychological complexity of his films.

The theme of 'Guilt and Innocence' often propels the plots of Hitchcock's films. From being falsely implicated in a crime they did not commit, like Richard Hannay in 'The 39 Steps' or Roger Thornhill in 'North by Northwest,' these protagonists find their world turned upside down, caught up in a web of intrigues and machinations they struggle to understand.

Another signature Hitchcock motif, used to amplify the theme of 'Guilt and Innocence,' is the plot device known as the 'MacGuffin,' an object or piece of information that drives the narrative. Though ostensibly significant to the plot, the actual nature of the 'MacGuffin' is often irrelevant to the movie's overall understanding. It merely serves as a catalyst, triggering the protagonist's actions and drawing them into perilous situations.

The motif of 'Duality and Deception' further intensifies the intricate narratives. Characters in Hitchcock's films often have dual natures or hidden aspects, from Norman Bates in 'Psycho' to the two seemingly ordinary tennis players in 'Strangers on a Train.' This motif goes hand-in-hand with the theme of 'Appearances Can Be Deceptive,' highlighting the contrast between the surface-level appearances of his characters and their hidden realities.

Hitchcock's films also frequently explore the theme of 'Obsession,' primarily through the eyes of his male protagonists. Whether Scottie's obsession with Madeleine in 'Vertigo' or Mark Rutland's fascination with Marnie in 'Marnie,' these obsessions spiral into dark and dangerous territories, blurring the lines between love and fixation.

Delving into these obsessions often leads to another recurring theme in Hitchcock's films: 'Madness and Sanity.' The line between sanity and insanity is frequently blurred. One could see this psychological tension in scenes such as Marion Crane's infamous shower scene in 'Psycho' or Charlotte's mental breakdown in 'Under Capricorn.'

The motif of 'The Wrong Man' is prevalent throughout Hitchcock's filmography. He revelled in placing an innocent protagonist in an unfamiliar, perilous situation. Hitchcock used this plot device to exhibit shared human fears of powerlessness and distrust of authority, showcasing the protagonist's evolution as they navigate these extreme circumstances.

'Fear of Heights' or acrophobia is a recurring motif in Hitchcock's films. In 'Vertigo', Scottie's acrophobia, both literal and metaphorical, forms an integral part of the narrative. This fear extends beyond the physical dread of heights, embodying the protagonist's psychological and emotional vulnerabilities.

The exceptional use of 'Staircases' is another motif that adds depth to Hitchcock's films. From ascending into danger in 'Psycho' to descending into madness in 'Vertigo', staircases often symbolize a transition or twist in the narrative journey of the characters, infusing dramatic tension.

Hitchcock also had a penchant for showcasing the motif of 'Eyes and Gaze.' His films often contain essential shots of eyes, either watching, being watched, invoking fear, or even inciting compassion. This visual emphasis on eyes carries the theme of 'Voyeurism,' reflecting on the audience's own participation in the act of viewing.

'Birds,' a recurrent motif in Hitchcock's films, carry various symbolic meanings. In 'The Birds,' they embody unpredictable, violent nature, while in 'Psycho,' taxidermy birds infer Norman Bates's predatory tendencies. This flexibility of symbolism is a testament to Hitchcock's prowess as a storyteller and visual poet.

In conclusion, Hitchcock's motifs were never mere decorative elements. They redefined conventional filmic symbolism, adding depth and psychological complexity. His fascination with human frailties, obsessions, fear, and guilt breathed life into these themes, creating timeless narratives that continue to provoke and captivate.

Examining these intricate themes and motifs opens up a new perspective in appreciating and interpreting the sheer depth of Alfred Hitchcock's cinematic genius. As we decode them, we gain deeper insights into his creative process and the art of storytelling itself.

Cinematographic Exploration

When exploring the cinematography of Alfred Hitchcock's filmography, the inquisition takes us deep into the heart of his genius. It's an adventurous journey filled with mystery and suspense, much like his movies. To savor the Hitchcockian experience, it is essential to delve deeper into the cinematic techniques he employed.

To most, Hitchcock was a master storyteller, but to others, he was an unparalleled cinematic experimenter. A significant part of his narrative voice was the savvy manipulation of visual elements. He used these elements to his advantage, remarkably grounding his narratives in the deliberate orchestration of these parts.

In the captivating confines of "Rear Window," one can't help but notice the use of perspective, an indispensable tool in Hitchcock's arsenal. While the movie unfolds from the perspective of a voyeur, it is Hitchcock's direction that makes the audience a part of this voyeuristic experience. The camera movements and angles mimic the protagonist's wheelchair-bound, peering outlook, making this a primary example of Hitchcock's command over the visual narrative.

The intuitive use of framing in "Rear Window" adds an interesting layer to the Hitchcockian narrative. The perspective shifts seamlessly between the story's inside and outside, creating a natural transition and flow within shots. This executes the polarities of the protagonist's confined and the lively external world with an immersive visual grammar that speaks directly to the viewers.

Hitchcock also paid significant attention to composition, making each frame a standalone artwork. Noteworthy examples span, for instance, across "Vertigo" and "North by

Northwest," where meticulous attention to detailing ornaments each shot, pushing the realms of conventional filmmaking.

During the meticulous analysis of "Vertigo," Hitchcock's use of colors and composition seems unmissable. A stark contrast is observed in the use of colors as the emotions of the characters progress through the film. Starting from soft pastels when all is well, the color scheme gets bolder, darker, hinting at the impending turmoil. This careful employment of color as a barometer of feelings made Hitchcock's storytelling visually appealing and emotionally stirring.

In "North by Northwest," the cinematographic principle of the "rule of thirds" has been used extensively, particularly in the iconic crop-duster scene. This use of the rule adds depth to the visuals, creating a complex and yet harmonious visual balance. The arid landscape takes two-thirds of the screen when Cary Grant is vulnerable and alone, dwarfed, and positioned in the lower third.

Similarly, in the Mount Rushmore sequence, the characters occupy a portion of the frame countered by the monument's immensity. Hitchcock's use of composition geniusly harmonizes the elements in the frame while rendering a powerful visual effect.

Next comes the exploration of Hitchcock's use of lighting and shadows, undoubtedly one of his signature styles. In the movie "Psycho," the use of high contrast lighting spoke volumes about the lurking danger and uncertainty. The ominous shadows, the dimly lit setting, were all calculated choices that amplified the suspense and tension in the narrative while insinuating the hidden darkness in the characters.

Another aspect worth noting is Hitchcock's pioneering use of camera movements. His "dolly zoom" in "Vertigo" created an unsettling visual effect that perfectly captured the protagonist's fear of heights and disorientation. The camera movement complemented the character's emotional state, effectively reflecting it on screen, hence creating a cinematic language to convey subjective experiences.

The iconic shower scene in "Psycho," with its fast cuts and unique camera angles, is representative of Hitchcock's experimental editing style. The rapid intercutting of shots, unusual camera movements, and the rhythmic crescendo of music results in a suspenseful cinematic masterpiece exuding a palpable sense of dread.

Alfred Hitchcock also harnessed the power of sound design to punctuate the suspense in his narratives. The absence of music in "The Birds," replacing it with electronically produced bird noises, heightened the viewers' unease, making it one of the unsung heroes in Hitchcock's basket of innovative cinematic techniques.

The cinematographic exploration of Alfred Hitchcock's work reveals his artistry, innovativeness, and unflinching resolve to push the envelope of filmmaking. The hallmark of Hitchcockian cinema is not only his refined visual vocabulary but also the inimitable ability to weave it within his narratives, making him a true auteur whose cinema still awakens awe and admiration.

By comprehensively analyzing Hitchcock's cinematic storytelling, we can better appreciate the depth of his craft and the legacy he left behind. His cinematic exploits continue to be a rich source of inspiration and a study in perfection for anyone willing to learn about moviemaking and its various facets, painting a glorious picture of cinema's golden age and an auteur par excellence.

Cultural Relevance

Alfred Hitchcock's "Rear Window" is more than just an exemplary piece of film-making; it is a popular culture phenomenon that is as relevant today as it was in the 1950s. The film's themes of voyeurism, isolation, and the infringement of privacy intersect with numerous contemporary cultural concerns, making it much more than a simple thriller. "Rear Window" gives us a glimpse into the time-period it was made and its cultural idiosyncrasies while also holding up a mirror to modern society, reflecting our significant preoccupations.

At a fundamental level, the film can be interpreted as a critique of the voyeuristic tendency in human nature, manifested significantly in today's age of social media and reality television. These platforms, just like the apartment complex in "Rear Window," offer individuals the opportunity to indulge their curiosity about other people's private lives without the guilt of intrusion. The escapism that Jeff experiences watching his neighbors is similar to scrolling through Instagram or watching a reality TV show, highlighting the timelessness of Hitchcock's work.

Furthermore, the film's exploration of female empowerment is surprisingly progressive. Lisa Fremont, played by Grace Kelly, initially seems to appear as a typical 1950s woman, devoted to her man and concerned with fashion. However, she evolves into a character who is independent, intelligent, and resourceful, significantly contrasting the stereotypical depiction of women at the time. Hitchcock presents a compelling case of female strength and defies the culture of the 1950s, creating a relevance that continues to resonate with audiences in the 21st century.

The film also grapples with the notion of urban isolation, a concept that is as pertinent now as it ever was. Despite living in close proximity to each other, the characters in "Rear Window" hardly communicate or show any sign of genuine companionship. Hitchcock uses this disconnect to comment on the alienation and loneliness prevalent in urban societies, which, despite technological advancements and social media platforms, is a significant issue in contemporary society too.

The film's relevance also extends to its examination of masculinity and disability. Jeff's immobility and dependence wrangle with the traditional idea of a male hero, giving the film a modern edge. This challenged notion of masculinity draws attention to changing societal standards, resonating with 21st-century culture as it struggles to redefine gender roles and expectations.

Hitchcock's portrayal of a community's apathy towards privacy, while pre-dating the age of smartphones and surveillance, is a compelling commentary on privacy invasion. The film's uncanny foresight about societies becoming increasingly comfortable with having their lives on display aligns eerily with the selfie culture and the comfort with which people share their lives on social platforms.

"Rear Window" stands not only as an extraordinary work of suspense and storytelling, but as a sociological artifact. It provides a snapshot of a specific time and place, yet it argues for themes that are universal and timeless. The film's characters may be set in the past, but their experiences and emotions continue to effect and resonate with audiences today, making "Rear Window" a timeless classic.

The movie's exploration of themes related to surveillance and the invasion of privacy also make it relevant in an era marked by anxiety about technology's effect on public and private boundaries. As citizens of the digital age, we grapple with these concerns daily, and "Rear Window" serves as an important touchstone for these dialogues.

Hitchcock uses "Rear Window" as a prism to offer commentary on societal norms and culture. The film continues to remain a cultural artifact that keeps influencing contemporary society, which is evident in numerous remakes and reinterpretations.

It's often said that good art holds up a mirror to society, reflecting its virtues and vices. If that's the case, it's fair to say that "Rear Window" serves as an eerily reflective and prescient mirror that continues to be as relevant today, if not more than when it was originally released.

It's this enduring applicability and its rich scholarly potential that places this movie at a prestigious standing in cinema history. "Rear Window," with its blend of a tightly woven narrative, impeccable cinematography, and rich sociocultural relevance, cements Hitchcock's stature as a filmmaker who was genuinely ahead of his time.

As we close this section, it's certainly clear that the cultural relevance of "Rear Window" can't be understated. From gender roles to consumer culture, Hitchcock's film continues to be a source of academic study and public fascination. This cultural analysis only enriches our understanding of Hitchcock's cinematic masterpiece, adding another layer to his complex, intriguing world of suspense and drama.

So, while Hitchcock may be the master of suspense, we can see through an analysis of "Rear Window" that his abilities extend far beyond just shocking and entertaining audiences. Hitchcock's sharp understanding of society's cultural and psychological landscape makes his films deeply interconnected with the world around them. These connections are what elevate "Rear Window" from being merely a window into the past, to a conduit of understanding the future.

Chapter 8: Unraveling "North by Northwest"

In "North by Northwest," Hitchcock employs a thrilling blend of plot twists, suspense, and romance to weave a complex narrative web of mistaken identities and intriguing pursuits. Cary Grant's character, mistaken for a nonexistent spy, becomes drawn into a perilous saga that carries him from the comforts of New York to the perilous heights of Mount Rushmore. Layered with suspenseful elements, viewers are pulled into iconic scenes such as the unnerving crop duster chase, where a hostile plane appears in the desolate fields and proceeds to pursue Grant's character. This scene is a masterclass in framing and editing, making full use of long shots to underscore the isolation of the character, and the sudden, jarring cuts to close-ups heightening the suspense. Hitchcock meticulously wields sound, often underscored through strategically placed silence, swinging the viewer between the realms of anxiety and relief. The expert marriage of these techniques builds an unrivaled tension that is characteristic of Hitchcock's work. The film's take on concepts of identity further complicates the narrative, adding a layer of depth that makes this thriller far more than just a cat and mouse chase. The characters' struggle with identity, mistaken or otherwise, coupled with the thrill-filled pursuit and the intense romance bubbling under the surface, gives the film a surreal and yet wholly immersive allure that stands as a testament to Hitchcock's unparalleled genius.

Plot Overview and Analysis

In "North by Northwest," the protagonist, Roger Thornhill, is mistakenly identified as George Kaplan, a fictional government agent created by the Central Intelligence Agency. Upon this mistaken identity, Thornhill is drawn into a world of espionage and danger, continually on the run from foreign agents. The story embodies the theme of mistaken identity, which is emphasized by the analysis of the plot and the cinematographic style of Hitchcock.

Roger Thornhill, an advertising executive, starts off as a self-centered and self-serving individual. But the advancing peril pushes him to transform into a more authentic, empathetic, and heroic figure, portraying Hitchcock's prevalent theme of transformation under coercion. His encounters include being pursued by a crop-dusting airplane in a desolate field and racing across the face of Mount Rushmore, engaging the audience with a thrilling adventure.

Hitchcock constructs the narrative architecture of fear and suspense throughout Thornhill's journey. There's a sense of constant pursuit that relentlessly drives the storyline. From Thornhill's abduction at the beginning to the climactic scene at Mount Rushmore, the audience is kept on their toes, always bracing for the unknown. Hitchcock's mastery of suspense is evidently present in this film.

The plot also weaves in a romantic storyline where Thornhill falls in love with a mysterious woman named Eve Kendall. As Thornhill navigates through the treacherous terrain of espionage, he is compelled to question his trust in Eve. The audience's perception of Eve changes throughout the film, as Hitchcock presents her as both an ally and a foe, sustaining the suspense.

As Hitchcock builds tension within the plot through the paranoia of Thornhill's life, "North by Northwest" heads towards the climax. The grand finale at Mount Rushmore, a symbol of American identity, not only serves to heighten the suspense but to also magnify the theme of false identity, reinforcing the overall plot thoroughly woven by Hitchcock.

From a cinematography standpoint, Hitchcock's "North by Northwest" is an outstanding example of cohesive visual storytelling. The use of cinematic techniques amplifies the film's impact such as framing, editing, and sound contributes to the overarching plot and themes.

Effective use of the camera frame is evident throughout the film; it often captures a sense of confinement, correlating with Thornhill's trapped condition. Hitchcock's clever cinematography manipulates visuals to subliminally convey the emotional state of the film's characters akin to the scene of Thornhill's solitary, doomed figure in the vast expanse of the fields, chased by a crop duster.

Hitchcock's editing style also plays a significant role in driving the story. As noted, the scene editing in the crop duster chase sequence is particularly gripping, maintaining suspense and tension. Additionally, Hitchcock's noteworthy silent scenes often juxtapose the intense moments, harnessing the power of contrast.

The distinctive characteristic of Hitchcock's films is the sound, playing a critical role in shaping the viewer's emotions. "North by Northwest" is no different. The use of non-diegetic sound, like background score, often augments suspense, while the strategic silence in specific scenes enhances suspense.

All these techniques culminate in several iconic scenes such as the Crop Duster and Mount Rushmore sequences. However, their significance isn't just visual spectacle but forms integral parts of the narrative infrastructure, serving Hitchcock's masterful storytelling.

Throughout the film, Hitchcock explores themes such as mistaken identity, transformation, pursuit, and trust via cleverly interwoven plot devices. Worth mentioning is the cynicism over Cold War-era intelligence agencies, adding to the film's historical context, further enriching the plot's setting.

While "North by Northwest" offers a riveting narrative filled with suspense and twists, it also elevates the cinematic techniques used, highlighting Hitchcock's innovative approach. These elements combined make it one of the seminal works in the espionage thriller genre.

Nevertheless, the beauty of Hitchcock's work lies not solely in its visual grandeur or plot intricacies, but also in the audience's ability to uncover layers of meaning through repeated viewing. "North by Northwest" continues to captivate each viewer with its deep narrative and technical prowess, reinforcing Hitchcock's legacy as the master of suspense.

In conclusion, Hitchcock's "North by Northwest" isn't just a seminal work in the espionage thriller genre, it also represents a pinnacle of Hitchcock's creative outpouring. From this detailed analysis of the plot and the accompanying cinematographic techniques, the intricacies of Hitchcock's craftsmanship are evident. This is a testament to his brilliance that continues to be revelled in, amongst film enthusiasts and scholars alike, even years after his time.

Iconic Scenes: The Crop Duster, Mount Rushmore

In "North by Northwest," Alfred Hitchcock masterfully crafted scenes that remain etched in the annals of cinematic history. Two memorable instances that bear repeating - the Crop Duster and Mount Rushmore sequences - warrant an analysis from a cinematography viewpoint.

Firstly, the Crop Duster sequence in an expansive, barren area of farmland is an embodiment of Hitchcock's brilliance. Let's delve into the reasons why. Upon first glance, the scene employs a masterful use of setting and geography to induce suspense. The protagonist, Roger Thornhill (Cary Grant), steps off a bus in a secluded landscape. The vast, infinite stretch of land and sky in all directions encapsulates his isolation and vulnerability.

What makes this scene unique in Hitchcock's work is the notable absence of conventional support structures - there are no tall buildings, no streets, merely a man stranded in a desolate field. This barren topography thus amplifies Thornhill's susceptibility and impending danger.

Another telling aspect of this sequence is the way Hitchcock manipulates time. Most of the scene is built around waiting, anticipation, and expectancy. There's a palpable sense of apprehension as Thornhill remains in a state of the uncertain, continuously checking his watch. Hitchcock brilliantly stretches it into a phenomenal suspense piece.

The camera movement and angles further intensify the plot's tension. The camerawork's dynamism displays Thornhill trying to flee from an oncoming crop-dusting plane. The low-angle shots of the plane symbolize an all-pervasive threat, while the more expansive high-angle shots emphasize Thornhill's vulnerability.

Last but not least, the use of diegetic sound in this scene deserves close scrutiny. Hitchcock cleverly omits non-diegetic, suspense-inducing music to enhance the authenticity. The harsh, uncontrollable sound of the plane's engine pairs with the unnerving quiet to accentuate the brewing terror.

Moving on to the Mount Rushmore sequence, it is yet another Hitchcock classic that challenges conventions by employing symbolism and innovative framing. The monument, representing America's power and grandeur, provides the backdrop for a nail-biting chase and combat encounter, turning it into a battleground.

In this scenario, Hitchcock forces us to witness the usually incredulous, monumental faces of the great American leaders overlook the unfolding drama. This clever visual metaphor reflects the absurdity and mystery underpinning the entire narrative.

We return here to Hitchcock's mastery in employing wide shots to create a sense of dangerous exposure. The protagonists' precarious climb across the stone faces of the presidents is expertly captured in wide, panoramic shots that amplify the dangerous height and sheer drop below.

In contrast, the director employs close-ups to unravel the intense emotions the characters experience in the face of danger. The expressions on Eve Kendall's (Eva Marie Saint) face as she navigates the treacherous mountainside are nothing short of captivating. The disparity between these wide-shots and close-ups heightens the suspense throughout the chase.

A review of the audio elements in the Mount Rushmore sequences is also insightful. Hitchcock's effective use of silence in the scene immediately before the chase creates a sense of calm before the storm. The interruption of this tranquility by the harsh, raging sound effects of the chase creates an abrupt contrast that amplifies the tension.

In conclusion, these two iconic sequences from "North by Northwest" exemplify Hitchcock's unparalleled ability to generate suspense by deftly employing a range of cinematographic elements. The Crop Duster and Mount Rushmore scenes remain timeless and influential, reminding us why Hitchcock is lauded as a master of cinematic suspense.

Cinematic Techniques: Framing, Editing, Sound

The grandeur of Hitchcock's films doesn't simply lie within their gripping plots or compelling characters, but also in his innovative use of framing, editing, and sound. These techniques, often overlooked in casual viewings, are an essential part of cinematic storytelling that manipulates audiences subconsciously. Let's delve into the specific ways Hitchcock used these techniques to shape narrative and induce suspense in his masterpiece, "North by Northwest."

Framing in Hitchcock's films functions as a means of control, guiding the viewer's gaze to certain elements within the scene. For instance, the wide-angle shots displaying vast, desolate landscapes, create a sense of isolation and vulnerability. The viewer feels the protagonist's alienation and fears his exposure to danger. By contrast, Hitchcock manifests empathy and intimacy towards his characters through close-ups, often in their moments of intense emotion or revelation. With framing, he carefully orchestrates where you should look and what you should feel.

The role of editing in Hitchcock's films is multifaceted and innovative. Rapid cutting intensifies the pace of a scene, giving an impression of urgency or confusion. For instance, in the sequence where Roger Thornhill (Cary Grant) is pursued by the crop duster, Hitchcock employs rapid cutting between wide shots of an expansive barren landscape and close-ups of Thornhill to heighten the feeling of danger. This effective technique unveils the immensity of his predicament and the escalating anticipation.

Yet, Hitchcock also knows when to rely on the power of a lingering, uninterrupted shot. He does this to allow the tension or absurdity of a situation to fully sink in with the audience. In the famous Mount Rushmore sequence, the long shots of Thornhill and Eve Kendall (Eva Marie Saint) precariously navigating the monument impels the gripping fear of heights and the ever-lurking danger.

Hitchcock's films are celebrated for their innovative use of sound. In "North by Northwest," he uses both diegetic and non-diegetic sound to enhance the plot's complexities and enrich the viewing experience. Diegetic sound, i.e., sound that can logically be heard by the characters, plays a crucial role in developing tension. The menacing buzz of the crop duster, the screeching brakes of a vehicle, or the echoing gunshots are all examples of diegetic sound perfections, which amplify the peril the characters face and accentuate suspense for viewers.

Non-diegetic sound, on the other hand, which refers to sources of sound not visible on the screen, is just as impactful. Bernard Herrmann's orchestral score underlines the dramatic tension, melancholy, or romantic moments of the film. It's as if the music puts into words what the characters can't express, guiding the audience's emotions throughout the narrative.

Yet, what is remarkable about Hitchcock is not just his creative use of these techniques, but his unique combination of them to maximize impact. One can observe this amalgamation in the iconic scene where Thornhill escapes from the auction room. Here, Hitchcock's framing leads the audience to alternate between Thornhill and the villainous Vandamm. The editing rhythm escalates as their confrontation intensifies, culminating in a gunshot that shocks the audience. Concurrently, the dramatic non-diegetic music builds anticipation, which abruptly ceases when the shot is fired, leaving the viewer with their own startled heartbeat and the diegetic ring of silence.

In many ways, Hitchcock's framing, editing, and sound techniques are protagonists in their own right—sometimes subtle, often audacious, always effective. They serve not just as stylistic embellishments but as narrative devices that shape the plot, develop characters, and kindle emotions. They are instruments of suspense, fear, and surprise, wielded masterfully by Hitchcock, culminating in a symphony of suspense that makes his films unforgettable.

To fully appreciate Hitchcock's technical genius, it's enlightening to watch "North by Northwest" with an analytic eye, observing these techniques in action. Each viewing can reveal a new layer, a previously overlooked nuance of framing, a subtle shift in the editing rhythm, or a key sound effect that changes how you perceive the scene.

Understandably, not everyone can be an expert in cinematography or master it overnight. But everyone can start to develop a distinctive eye for these techniques. All it takes is a keen sense of observation and an open mind to appreciate the profound effects these techniques have on both a film's narrative and our emotional response.

Looking at "North by Northwest" through this lens, one realizes Hitchcock's true proficiency as a filmmaker. Yes, he has the knack for crafting compelling stories and unforgettable characters, but his utter mastery over the craft of filmmaking, his ability to manipulate the technical elements of cinema—framing, editing, and sound—to his advantage, is what makes him a true auteur in the landscape of cinema.

So as you watch "North by Northwest," and indeed any other Hitchcock film, make it an adventure. Venture into the world of framing, descend into the depths of editing, and brave the excitements of sound. But above all, remember that these aren't just tools in Hitchcock's hand—they are his voice, his expression, manifest on the silver screen.

Let's dissect, analyze, and appreciate his technical virtuosity as we foster a deeper sense of admiration for one of the greatest filmmakers of all time—Alfred Hitchcock.

Themes and Symbols: Identity, Pursuit, Romance

The thematic exploration of Alfred Hitchcock's films is primarily focused on the concept of identity, the idea of pursuit, and the complexities of romance. These three themes not only intertwine within individual films but also resonate across Hitchcock's entire body of work, underlying the fundamental emotions, motives, and arcs of the characters, as well as the plot.

Hitchcock's portrayal of identity is often linked to complexity and uncertainty. This ambiguity manifests itself in his characters, who often grapple with their perceived identities versus their true selves. In "North by Northwest," Roger Thornhill, the protagonist, is mistaken for a US government agent by foreign spies. This mistaken identity propels the plot and character development throughout the film. The dichotomy between who we are and who others perceive us to be is Hitchcock's exploration of the human psyche and personal identity.

In Hitchcock's scope, identity isn't merely confined to individuals but also stretches to represent entire societies and cultures. His films often challenge social identity norms, questioning established conventions and challenging common stereotypes. The use of transgressive characters, like the titular Norman Bates in "Psycho," serves to subvert societal expectations about identity, especially those related to gender and psychological health.

Next to the theme of identity, Hitchcock's films prominently feature the motive of pursuit. Often, the narrative is driven as much by an individual's pursuit of something - or someone - as it is by the external circumstances challenging them. The relentless chase orchestrates the suspense, whether it is Thornhill's desperate evasion from his mysterious persuers in "North by Northwest" or Detective Scottie's compulsive pursuit of Madeleine in "Vertigo".

However, Hitchcock's perspective of pursuit isn't confined to mere plot devices. It is strongly tied to larger existential questions of meaning, purpose and obsession. The act of pursuit symbolizes a deeper longing, an insatiable desire to attain the unattainable. Whether it's the pursuit of truth, justice, an unreachable love interest, or even oneself, Hitchcock masterfully portrays the futile and self-destructive nature of such pursuits.

Lastly, the theme of romance in Hitchcock's films notably revolves around fatal attraction, tragic love, and romantic obsession. His characters are often caught in tortuous love affairs, tumultuous relationships, or one-sided infatuations.

This is starkly visible in "Vertigo," where Scottie falls obsessively in love with Madeleine, only to face heartbreak and disillusionment.

The dangerous romance that underlines Hitchcock's films often serves as a catalyst for his characters' actions and eventual doom. However, it also shows his characters' vulnerability and desire for affection, even in the face of impending danger. It is in this complex junction of romance, danger, and human instincts that Hitchcock revels, adding more psychological depth to his films.

Hitchcock also uses an abundance of symbols to depict identities, pursuits, and romances. Mirrors often symbolize duality and deception, reflecting characters' struggle with their identities. Stairs and heights are frequently used to symbolize pursuit and the resulting danger, often encountered in precarious situations. Birds often symbolize impending doom or are used as harbingers of tragic romances—making one reminisce about the unnerving bird attacks in "The Birds" or the haunting gaze of Norman's stuffed birds in "Psycho".

Thus, Hitchcock weaves together these three major themes and symbols in a unique narrative style that keeps the audience on the edge of their seats. His films invite viewers to engage in a deeper exploration of the characters' psyches: their identities, pursuits, and romances, and the toll these take on their lives.

Hitchcock's artistry lies not just in the memorable themes and symbols he employs, but also in the careful construction of a cinematic language that emphasizes these elements subtly yet consistently. As we move further into the unknown realms of Hitchcock's world, we will uncover more about how the director used these elements to create his timeless masterpieces.

From the flawed everyman plunged into a world of chaos and identity crisis to the relentless pursuit often leading to a tragic downfall, and the complex, doomed romances, Hitchcock exhibited an unparalleled understanding of human nature and its dark complexities. And it is this profound understanding that makes his films continue to resonate with audiences even today.

Chapter 9: Lesser-Known Masterpieces

As we journey deeper into the landscape of Hitchcock's creative genius, let's turn the spotlight onto some of his lesser-known masterpieces that epitomize his filmmaking prowess. Films like "Rope," "Strangers on a Train," and "Dial M for Murder," aren't quite to the same level of widespread acclaim as some of his other works, yet they are treasures worth delving into. "Rope" for instance, with its seemingly continuous shot approach, pushes the envelope on conventional film techniques. Hitchcock experimented with extended takes, effectively painting a picture of real-time suspense, a predilection he maintained throughout his career. Then, there's "Strangers on a Train," a story built on suspense and moral ambiguity. Hitchcock flexed his narrative and visual muscles in an alternative way here, utilizing a tennis match as an element of mounting tension and cross-cutting sequences to juxtapose parallel chains of events. Last, but not least, "Dial M for Murder" presents a masterclass in suspense through confined space. Hitchcock was able to craft a thrilling tale of deceit and murder through meticulous camera work and lighting within a single apartment set. Despite standing in the shadows of other acclaimed films, these lesser-known works underscore Hitchcock's versatility in employing varied cinematic techniques. Their detailed analysis helps us further understand his unique storytelling style and offers learning opportunities for cinephiles and aspiring filmmakers seeking a flair of suspense in their narrative craft.

Rope

For many, "Rope" remains a lesser-known gem in Alfred Hitchcock's esteemed repertoire. This film features a taste of Hitchcock's audacious ambition and unique approach to cinematography, making it a must for the enthusiasts of film and Hitchcock. The movie is as audacious and unique as the techniques he employed to shoot it.

"Rope" was Hitchcock's first color film, released in 1948. It's a brooding, philosophical thriller that employs long-takes, a virtually single set, and intense psychological drama that hinges on a continuous 80-minute shot. This format breaks away from more traditional methods of film editing and dramaturgy, allowing the tension to build in real-time mimicking the temporal unity of Greek drama.

Hitchcock's stand-out use of cinematography—an experimental approach making "Rope" seem like a play rather than a movie—is captivating. The camera becomes a character within the film, seemingly acting as the eyes of Brandon and Philip (the two main characters). The lack of multiple locations and camera cuts removes any sense of a safety barrier between the viewer and the horror unfolding on screen, enhancing the unsettling atmosphere.

The film is also notable for its groundbreaking use of lighting. Hitchcock wanted his audience to feel the passage of time, so he had his team create lighting setups mimicking both dusk and night, constructing a continuous storyline. As the movie progresses, the light changes subtly, the way it does over an evening. This pioneering use of lighting, combined with minimal set changes, creates an unparalleled sense of realism.

Despite being a gruesome murder plot, there's no overt violence in "Rope". Instead, the horror resides in the idea of the crime, the motivation behind it, and the audacity of the killers to host a dinner party immediately afterwards. Throughout the film, the titular rope—a seemingly insignificant object—is frequently reintroduced as a silent reminder of the brutal murder committed by the young protagonists, creating a tangible tension that remains at high intensity till the end.

The unique conception of "Rope", particularly Hitchcock's experimental filming techniques, was not universally understood or appreciated at its release. It was only over subsequent years, as filmmakers began to push against traditional boundaries, that the subtlety of the experiment and its impact on audience experience came to be appreciated.

"Rope" is a demonstration of Hitchcock's ability to make viewers feel uncomfortable through his masterful manipulation of time and pace. His use of confined settings and unbroken shots allows him to ramp up the tension and suspense, ultimately eliciting audience unease. Through the lens of "Rope", Hitchcock explores his recurring theme of guilt, effectively highlighting how guilt can reveal itself in the most unexpected situations.

The film's premise, characters, and relentless tension reflect the cinematic techniques and thematic concerns that would come to define Hitchcock's career. By applying these techniques to a simple and chilling plot, Hitchcock constructs a riveting film experience despite limiting himself to a single location.

In conclusion, "Rope," with its unconventional cinematography and storytelling methods, stands as a testament to Hitchcock's boundless innovation and creativity. It remains an invaluable filmography piece for both Hitchcock enthusiasts and students of the art of cinema, demonstrating the power of expansive imagination within confined spaces.

Strangers on a Train

In the realm of lesser-known yet incredibly crafted Hitchcock masterpieces, "Strangers on a Train" stands out. This 1951 film is a fine blend of suspense, drama, and meticulous cinematography that reflects Hitchcock's filmmaking prowess. Expertly composed frames, hidden meanings behind camera angles and innovative lighting techniques came together to create a movie that echoes Hitchcock's signature style.

Based on Patricia Highsmith's debut novel, the plot revolves around two strangers who meet on a train. One, a tennis player named Guy, wants to rid himself of his shrewish wife, while the other, a wealthy eccentric named Bruno, wants his father dead. The casual yet sinister proposal of an exchange of murders – Bruno killing Guy's wife and Guy murdering Bruno's father – sets the stage for a relentless psychological thriller.

One of the film's most striking scenes, the murder of Guy's wife, Miriam, reflected through Bruno's sunglass lenses, demonstrated Hitchcock's ability to create drama through cinematography. Using a long shot from Bruno's perspective, Hitchcock brilliantly framed the murder within the glasses, thus emphasizing the voyeuristic undertone and intensifying the horror.

Annotated for its extensive use of parallel editing, "Strangers on a Train" exploits this technique to compare and contrast the lives of Guy and Bruno. The recurring theme of doubles, suggested visually through recurring images of mirrored items and actions, also adds depth to the film. The meticulous mirroring of both characters underscores the chilling possibility of evil even in average people's psyche.

Hitchcock made great use of his signature MacGuffin in "Strangers on a Train". Here, the lighter inscribed with Guy's initials and a tennis racquet plays this part. The lighter's journey, lost, found and finally used as incriminating evidence against Guy, adds an extra layer of suspense to the narrative.

Ambiguously lighting the main characters is another cinematography element of distinction in this Hitchcock film. Guy's character, initially lit to appear innocent, becomes increasingly clouded in shadow as his implication in the murder plot deepens. Bruno, on the other hand, initially appears dark and sinister but is later seen bathed in soft light, infusing his psychopathic character with an unsettling charm.

Undeniably, Hitchcock's choice of camera angles in "Strangers on a Train" adds a dramatic element to the film. Hitchcock extensively used low-angle shots, especially in scenes featuring Bruno, emphasizing his dominance and malign nature.

The famous carousel scene, considered one of the most thrilling in Hitchcock's filmography, exemplifies his exceptional skill to combine camera movement, editing and sound. The revolving carousel, the escalating tension, the sharp editing cuts, the extreme close-ups, and the harsh, non-diegetic sounds of the spinning carousel create a climax filled with suspense and panic.

"Strangers on a Train", while possibly lesser-known, is by no means a lesser film. Its innovative cinematography elements, combined with a gripping plot and complex characters, make it a must-watch for Hitchcock enthusiasts. Its influence on subsequent thrillers is undeniable, making it one of the fine examples of Hitchcock's unparalleled cinematic genius.

As we continue to explore Hitchcock's films, we'll uncover more such gems of his cinematography. Our journey takes us next to another of his lesser-known classics, "Dial M for Murder".

Dial M for Murder

In an exploration of Hitchcock's masterpiece, "Dial M for Murder" each scene is meticulously crafted, pushing the boundaries of what a thriller could accomplish visually. It is within this film that viewers experience Hitchcock's true genius in creating tension and intrigue through skilforceful cinematography.

The film uses a limited set, primarily shot in an apartment, but yet, Hitchcock's camera work makes the space feel expansive and filled with dread. The close-ups are frequently used to bring attention to crucial objects - keys, scissors, or a phone. This not only heightens tension but also demonstrates the importance of each element in a scene, increasing the audience's anticipation.

Ingenuity is demonstrated to the fullest in the scene where Grace Kelly's character is attacked. Hitchcock employs a technique of shifting the audience's point of view from a bystander in the opening act to the assailant's perspective in the closing moments. This altering perception intensifies the emotional impact of the murder attempt, making it one of the film's most memorable moments.

The use of color in "Dial M for Murder" is another subtle element that Hitchcock well utilizes. Deep reds register the intensity of the plot and underscore the themes of passion, animosity, and murder. It pervades the costumes and the set, reinforcing the dangerous motives and highlighting the impending doom.

Lighting, as well, adds a notable narrative layer within the film. Hitchcock uses chiaroscuro, a lighting technique from the film noir genre, to create pronounced shadows within a scene. This not only dramatizes the visual environment but also pushes the narrative forward, pointing to the hidden secrets and nuances of the characters.

The clever camera angles and movements within "Dial M for Murder" cannot be overlooked. Hitchcock frequently used low-angle shots that helped to exaggerate character's emotions and to convey shifts in power dynamics. His mastery of visual storytelling was reflected in these well crafted shots.

Moreover, the use of sound— and the lack thereof— is vital to the film's suspenseful atmosphere. Moments of silence often precede the most action-packed scenes, escalating the sense of suspense and keeping the audience on the edge of their seats.

In dialing 'M' for his murder plot, Hitchcock employed an exciting balance of space, color, camera angles, and dramatic sound to create a captivating masterpiece. The film still stands as a testament to Hitchcock's ability to turn the technical aspects of filmmaking into elements of suspense, intrigue, and tension.

By focusing on the technique and delivery used in this film, it's clear that Hitchcock was a master at utilizing key elements of cinematography to drive the narrative and create thrilling suspense. The dissection of "Dial M for Murder" aids in understanding Hitchcock's techniques and his pioneering influence on the thriller genre.

Ultimately, Hitchcock's "Dial M for Murder" is a cinematographic symphony— a perfectly arranged set of instruments all playing together to create a grand spectacle. It is a testament to Hitchcock's craft, proving why he's rightly deemed the 'Master of Suspense'.

Analysis and Techniques

Taking a detailed look at Alfred Hitchcock's work, it becomes clear that suspense was his primary tool, but he also thrived through the use of a plethora of deliberate techniques. Lighting, camera angles, auditory cues, and pacing were all methodical inclusions that amplified his storytelling prowess.

The fundamental framework of Hitchcock's films relied heavily on the use of mise en scène. This term represents everything the camera sees within a scene and was manipulated masterfully by Hitchcock to create atmosphere, tension and expectation. Elements such as props, color, acting, and setting were all used to construct an intricate sense of mise en scène in his works.

Camera angles were another area where Hitchcock demonstrated a distinct prowess. The brilliance of shots in "North by Northwest" or "Rear Window" exemplify his knack for utilizing perspective to produce tension. By employing unique and often intimate camera angles, he managed to invoke a voyeuristic sense in the audience; an intentional decision that raised the levels of suspense exponentially.

The lighting in Hitchcock's films also played a significant role. He was particularly adept at utilizing shadows and darkness to create a sense of fear and foreboding. He made great use of chiaroscuro lighting, a technique where the stark contrast between light and dark shadows created a dramatic ambiance. This helped augment both the physical and psychological aspects of his films.

Truly a master of foreshadowing, Alfred Hitchcock employed various subtle cues to hint at the climax or twist that was yet to come. These could be visual, like a peculiar object in the background, or auditory like the ominous sound of a ticking clock. The purpose of this was to create an undercurrent of tension that kept the viewer on the edge of their seat.

Hitchcock's use of pacing and narrative rhythm formed another cornerstone of his filmmaking techniques. He demonstrated unmatched control over the flow of his films, knowing when to build tension and when to break it. Hitchcock knew precisely how to manage the ebb and flow of a storyline to sustain viewer engagement and deliver shocks at the most opportune time.

In terms of editing, Hitchcock was a master at using cuts and transitions to mislead his audience. His signature technique - the "Hitchcock Zoom" or "Vertigo effect" - is a perfect example of this. This trick involves zooming in while simultaneously moving the camera backwards, creating a disorienting effect that mirrors the protagonist's mental state.

Manipulating viewer's emotions was another notable skill. In "Psycho", Hitchcock mastered the technique of misdirection through the use of the MacGuffin. This term, coined by Hitchcock himself, refers to a plot device that serves as a false lead, ultimately superseded by the real crux of the story.

This served to keep the viewers anticipating something entirely different from what was eventually revealed.

With sound design, Hitchcock employed auditory cues not merely for atmosphere but as storytelling devices. He understood the importance of silence, and how its use could convey tension just as much as dramatic music could. The shower scene in "Psycho", where the only sound is that of the running water and the dreadful screeching of the knife, is a classic example.

He also made a point of utilizing certain colors to symbolize various elements within his films. For instance, in "Vertigo", the color green was used to symbolize the past and the eerie, dreamlike state that plagues its protagonist. Similarly, in "Rope" different colors and hues were employed to create a sense of the passage of time.

In front of the camera, the characters in Hitchcock's films often portrayed a duality of roles – revealing their 'double identities' through his carefully crafted narratives. Often, the villain of the film is initially introduced as a charming, amiable character in a stark contrast to their true chilling nature.

Hitchcock's films also acted as social commentaries, subtly addressing contemporary issues and attitudes. Be it the post-war paranoia in "North by Northwest", or the prevalent patriarchal norms in "Rear Window", Hitchcock had his own unique way of weaving these societal reflections into his narratives.

Lastly, the nature of his storylines often put ordinary, unsuspecting individuals in extraordinary circumstances, showcasing the unpredictable and precarious nature of life itself. Hitchcock excelled in creating an investing narrative around the idea of 'the wrong man accused', further adding to his signature suspenseful style.

Thus, our tour of Hitchcock's techniques and their brilliant execution in some of his greatest films acts as a primer to understanding the magic of his storytelling. From understanding his genius, one can take away invaluable lessons for creating compelling narratives that keep audiences completely engrossed till the end.

In conclusion, Hitchcock's techniques were innovatively used to build suspense and intensify the viewer's experience. With mis en scène, lighting, sound, and much more, Hitchcock masterfully crafted each scene to advance his narrative and evoke the desired emotions. These cinematic techniques are not only useful to analyze Hitchcock's films, but also serve as essential lessons for budding filmmakers and cinema enthusiasts to learn from.

Legacy and Learning

Considering the vast oeuvre of impressive films Hitchcock directed, it is evident that he did not only create movies, but he left a palpable and deeply influential legacy that is not easily summarized. His work traverses time, with each generation finding something to connect with in his films and learn from his innovative techniques. In this chapter, we will dive into what the cinematic world has gleaned from the masterful director and discuss the impact he continues to have on filmmakers and filmgoers worldwide.

Hitchcock's movies were unique and ground-breaking, and his influence extends to many facets of cinema. He ushered in new forms of storytelling through suspense, revolutionized the use of sound, and created unforgettable visual motifs. His technical innovations were just as influential as his storytelling techniques, and the techniques he deployed are profoundly educational for any aspiring filmmaker or cinematographer, showing us new ways to see the world through a lens.

Hitchcock's influence has beyond the screen itself, into the realm of film criticism and analysis. His work has challenged generations of film students in interpreting and understanding the scope of his vision and his command over the medium. His work is a treasure trove of lessons that go beyond the specifics of craft and delve into the nature of storytelling, human psychology, and the art of suspense.

The palpable tension and accompanying unpredictability in Hitchcock's narrative structure has undoubtedly benefitted the thriller and horror genre. Mastering the art of suspense, Hitchcock's movies remain prime examples of how to craft a gripping narrative that steadily builds tension and intrigue. Film aficionados can learn the art of managing pacing and suspense from studying his oeuvre, a teaching that is invaluable in any cinematic genre.

One of Hitchcock's most significant contributions to cinema is undeniably his innovative use of sound. He used sound as a tool to induce fear and prolong suspense, turning it into a character of its own. From the screeching violins in "Psycho" to the silence in "The Birds", sound in Hitchcock's movies was always used with purpose and intent. This unconventional use of sound is an aspect that many filmmakers have since adopted and refined to suit their own narrative styles.

Film students and enthusiasts can also derive enormous inspiration from Hitchcock's avant-garde approach to cinematography. Be it his unique shot frames, exploration of camera angles or the way he made lighting work to his advantage – Hitchcock's keen eye and audacious creativity set a spectacular example for filmmakers to draw from.

The concept of MacGuffin, a term coined by the great director himself, is another lesson for film enthusiasts. The idea that a seemingly vital plot element, an object or goal, can be irrelevant to the overall story was novel when Hitchcock introduced it, forever changing the way storytellers weave their narratives.

Even Hitchcock's lesser-known films serve as educational tools. These films, despite not garnering as much commercial success, were every bit as innovative and groundbreaking. 'Rope', for instance, is a masterclass in how to use a single setting effectively, while 'Dial M for Murder' provides an illuminating study into the use of 3D in film.

Hitchcock was also famous for his collaboration. His relationships with actors, writers and composers are legendary, and these partnerships played a pivotal role in the success of his films. The mutual respect and understanding between Hitchcock and his collaborators is something aspiring filmmakers and cinephiles can learn from.

Appreciating Hitchcock's filmography also requires an understanding of his ability to reflect societal norms and mores of his time. One of the reasons his films continue to resonate today is because of the timeless quality in them. Even films like 'Rear Window', which is set in a bygone era, manage to connect with audiences because of the universal human experiences and emotions that Hitchcock depicted.

Hitchcock's unmatched ability to tap into universal fears and anxieties is another notable facet of his legacy. He could captivate audiences by inviting them into a world of suspense and uncertainty. This skill helps create lasting images and scenes that remain etched in public consciousness, such as the infamous shower scene in 'Psycho'. This knack for creating memorable scenes is worth emulation by filmmakers.

As we delve into the legacy of Hitchcock, it becomes clear that his influence on cinema is immense and continues to be part of filmmaking discourse. His body of work offers countless lessons in filmmaking techniques, narrative storytelling, and the manipulation of audience emotions.

His work, so rich, layered, and visually stunning, is a testament to his genius and remains a shining example of why Alfred Hitchcock will always be remembered as one of the most influential directors in the history of cinema. As we reflect on his legacy, we recognize that, through his work, we learn about film, about storytelling, about the human mind, and about ourselves.

Although Alfred Hitchcock passed away over four decades ago, his cinematic legacy is still growing. New generations of filmmakers, critics, and viewers continue discovering his filmography and learning from his trailblazing contributions. For future film enthusiasts, Hitchcock's legacy serves not only as a foundation to understand the past but also as a compass to navigate the future of cinema.

Chapter 10: Hitchcock and His Collaborators

The magic of Hitchcock's cinema wasn't simply the result of one man's genius; it was a collaboration between the master himself and a host of talented individuals. Much of his filmography's charm came from the incredible performances by accomplished actors and actresses—an illustrious list that includes James Stewart, Grace Kelly, Cary Grant, and Tippi Hedren, among others—each artist adding an inimitable facet to Hitchcock's visions of suspense. However, this collaborative symphony went beyond the realm of acting, and a significant portion of Hitchcock's cinematic palette was painted by some of the most prolific writers and composers of the era. The likes of Joseph Stefano, Françoise Truffaut, and John Michael Hayes contributed to the twisting narratives and memorable dialogues that adorned Hitchcock's filmography. Long-standing collaborator Bernard Herrmann's haunting scores, from the infamous "Psycho" strings to "Vertigo's" eerie love theme, became integral parts of the Hitchcockian experience. The successful synergy between Hitchcock and his collaborators formed a formidable unit, proving there's no 'i' in 'team,' even in the fiercely individualistic world of film artistry.

Actors and Actresses

Alfred Hitchcock, considered the undisputed master of cinematic suspense, had a knack for casting the most fitting actor or actress for his filmic ventures. His movies are iconic not only for their thrills, chills, and innovative techniques, but also for the unforgettable performances by so many accomplished actors and actresses. They brought Hitchcock's vision to life, adding depth and nuance to his well-woven stories of mystery and suspense.

His use of recurring actors and actresses, like Cary Grant and James Stewart, lent a sort of continuity to Hitchcock's filmography. Having these consistent players allowed Hitchcock to experiment with a variety of roles and character arcs while maintaining a level of predictability behind the scenes. The artists became trusted collaborators, understanding Hitchcock's creative rhythm and meeting his distinct standards.

Cary Grant, an urbane, charismatic actor, starred in four of Hitchcock's films. His roles ranged from a falsely accused man in 'North by Northwest' to a retired cat burglar in 'To Catch a Thief.' Grant exemplified Hitchcock's penchant for charming, but flawed heroes who are thrust into extraordinary circumstances. His suave demeanor and natural humor simultaneously put the audience at ease and enhanced the suspense.

James Stewart, another stalwart of Hitchcock's films, offered audiences a relatable protagonist with his everyman persona. His memorable roles include a wheelchair-bound photographer in 'Rear Window' and an acrophobic detective in 'Vertigo.' Stewart's likability secured viewer investment in his character's plight, a quality Hitchcock exploited to amp up the suspense and surprise twists.

Beyond these male leads, Hitchcock had an eye to create roles for women that were rich in complexity and intrigue. Actresses like Kim Novak, Ingrid Bergman, and Janet Leigh challenged the norms of their time with performances of extraordinary depth and emotional resonance.

Kim Novak, known for her famous double role in 'Vertigo,' embodied Hitchcock's ideal of the 'blonde ice queen.' Her dual portrayal of Madeleine and Judy illustrates Hitchcock's fascination with female duplicity and male obsession.

Ingrid Bergman starred in three Hitchcock films — 'Spellbound,' 'Notorious,' and 'Under Capricorn.' In 'Notorious,' playing a woman torn between love and duty, she gives a gripping performance that grasps the audience's sympathy. Hitchcock would often push her to her emotional limits to create compelling scenes.

Janet Leigh's performance in 'Psycho' is forever etched in cinema history. As Marion Crane, she embodies both a troubled thief and an innocent victim. Her iconic shower scene, though lasting less than three minutes, is perhaps one of cinema's most disturbing and indelible moments.

Dame Judith Anderson gave an unforgettable performance as the sinister housekeeper in 'Rebecca.' Her chilling portrayal of Mrs. Danvers, struggling between sorrow and a venomous resentment, was praised immensely, proving yet again Hitchcock's knack for uncovering layer upon layer of complex human behaviors and motivations.

Tippi Hedren, discovered by Hitchcock himself, performed in 'The Birds' and 'Marnie.' The roles, especially in 'The Birds,' allowed Hedren to showcase a range of emotions under duress, navigating through an eerie and tumultuous world. Hitchcock utilized her abilities, further contributing to his legacy of suspense.

The genius of Hitchcock though did not just lie in casting great actors. He utilized them as cinematic elements within his films, treating them as part of the mise-en-scène. They were not just players within his stories; they were tools in his toolbox, instrumental in striking the right emotional chords with his audience.

Through strategic casting, meticulous direction, and stunning character development, Alfred Hitchcock was able to elicit performances that defined careers, shaped the horror and suspense genre, and continue to leave audiences breathless. This brilliant use of his actors and actresses is one of the many reasons Hitchcock's films remain timeless in their impact and sheer entertainment.

It is thus important to understand that Hitchcock's genius was not in his method but in his madness - a madness where James Stewart could transform into a neighborly peeping tom, Cary Grant into an everyday hero, and Janet Leigh into everyone's worst nightmare. He blurred the lines between saint and sinner, right and wrong, reality and fantasy, using his actors and actresses as the medium to transmit this bizarre fusion to his audience. And they were more than up for the task.

Here we conclude our exploration of Hitchcock's trusted collaborators, his actors and actresses. In our next chapter, we'll delve into another integral part of Hitchcock's cinematic brilliance - his writers and composers. From the eloquently dark narratives to the hair-raising scores, we'll unpack how Hitchcock's relationships with these creatives significantly impacted the evolution of his style and the success of his films.

Writers and Composers

In this section, we delve into the gifted minds of the writers and composers who accompanied Hitchcock on his extraordinary journey, helping breathe life into his groundbreaking films.

The name Alfred Hitchcock is often synonymous with suspense and horror. Yet, beneath the thrill and the chills lie compelling narratives and unforgettable musical scores that elevated his films to unforgettable masterpieces. The individuals responsible for these vital elements were crucial members of Hitchcock's production team.

Let's begin with the writers. Hitchcock worked with a wide range of scribes, each contributing a unique edge to his storytelling style. He had a knack for recognizing talent and nurtured it accordingly. Among the most prominent was Alma Reville, Hitchcock's wife, who played a crucial role in shaping his films. Her influence extended beyond her credited work, often providing unaccredited contributions that added depth to Hitchcock's story arcs.

Another notable writer who worked on classic Hitchcock films was Joseph Stefano. Known for his work on Psycho, his stark and chilling dialogues played a vital role in distinguishing this classic film. Stefano's writing style can be described as intense and arresting; it immediately commanded the viewer's attention and heightened the iconic suspense Hitchcock revelled in.

Other writers of note include Evan Hunter, whose work on *The Birds* brought forth a seeming innocence, lulling the viewer into complacency before the sudden, dramatic onslaught. John Michael Hayes, who scripted *Rear Window*, is also worthy of mention, as his careful, calculated dialogue meticulously elucidated character deeper layers, complementing Hitchcock's visual storytelling.

Turning to the composers, it is impossible to ignore the indelible impact of Bernard Herrmann. Herrmann's work with Hitchcock revolutionized film scores, providing an inherent psychological component that ramped up the tension beautifully. His starkly tragic score for *Vertigo* remains as impressive today as it was on its release.

The disconcerting strings of *Psycho* were also Herrmann's composition. It's a theme that has haunted nightmares and symbolized terror for generations, becoming an integral synonym for fear in cinema. The composer's ability to meld sound with emotion was nothing short of astounding and played a significant role in augmenting Hitchcock's suspenseful forays.

Another important name in Hitchcock's musical roster was Dimitri Tiomkin. His compositions for *Strangers on a Train* and *Dial M for Murder* complemented Hitchcock's suspense-infused storytelling with calculated musical pacing juxtaposed with moments of thoughtful silence.

An often understated contributor was Franz Waxman, whose luminous score for *Rear Window* added lightness and melody to an otherwise claustrophobic atmosphere. Waxman's combination of lighthearted tunes with creeping suspense reflected Hitchcock's deceptive approach to story unravelling.

On a different, yet no less effective note, Miklós Rózsa's work on *Spellbound* made use of the early electronic instrument, the theremin, creating an eerie, distinctive quality that contributed to the film's unsettling ambiance. Rózsa brought a different flavor into Hitchcock's world, showcasing the director's eagerness to embrace innovation.

The synergy of these incredible individuals and their unique talents undoubtedly played a strong part in making Hitchcock's films the gemstones of cinema. From insightful dialogue and narrative depth to evocative scores that seeped into the subconscious, these writers and composers acted as the left and right hand of Hitchcock's narrative direction, contributing significantly to creating the immersive worlds that make watching a Hitchcock film such a thrilling experience.

While Hitchcock's directorial genius unquestionably played a decisive role in his films, this section aims to remember and champion the importance of writers and composers in constructing the cinematic experiences we cherish today.

We've explored a summary of talent and creativity on display in Hitchcock's team. Now, let's examine in detail the influence and synergy that resulted from these collaborations in the next chapter.

Influence and Synergy

The magic of cinema isn't just in the images we see on the screen, but it is truly a synergy of many elements working together; a collaborative effort that involves a multitude of individual talents. And in the case of Alfred Hitchcock, synergy and influence played an immensely integral role in the creation of his iconic films. In this section, I will delve into Hitchcock's relationships with his collaborators and the influence these partnerships had on his cinematic works.

We can't talk about Hitchcock's works without acknowledging Joan Harrison's substantial influence. One of his vital early collaborators, Harrison's career paralleled Hitchcock's rise as a master of suspense cinema. While Hitchcock had his distinctive directorial style, Harrison complemented it with her excellent screenwriting abilities. Their collaborations bore fruit in the form of classics like "Rebecca" and "Suspicion".

On the other hand, Hitchcock's collaboration with the composer Bernard Herrmann led to some of the most iconic film scores of all time. It's hard to imagine the shower scene in "Psycho" without Herrmann's screeching violin composition amplifying the terror. Hitchcock himself acknowledged, "33% of the effect of Psycho was due to the music". A testament to the importance of synergy in creating cinematic masterpieces.

Another key contributor to Hitchcock's films was his frequent collaborating cinematographer, Robert Burks. His ability to translate Hitchcock's psychological narratives into visual poetry was crucial in films like "Vertigo" and "Rear Window". His keen eye for detail and understanding of Hitchcock's vision made him an indispensable part of the craft.

Costume designer Edith Head and Hitchcock shared an unspoken language that translated onto the screen with remarkable accuracy. From creating Edna's austere get-up in "The Birds" to giving "To Catch a Thief" its stylish glamour, Head's understanding of Hitchcock's desired narrative visually expressed through wardrobe became a definitive part of his storytelling.

Rounding out Hitchcock's cadre of frequent collaborators were his go-to film editors, George Tomasini and Alma Reville, Hitchcock's own wife. Their crucial role cannot be understated, with their flawless editing skills driving Hitchcock's suspenseful sequences, amplifying tension, and so conveying his vision.

The women protagonists of Hitchcock's films have always been strong, progressive despite the era's societal norms. This was heavily influenced by the women in his life, particularly his wife, Alma, who was a dynamic, strong-willed woman. Through her, Hitchcock included powerful women characters in his films, breaking stereotypes, and stepping away from the confines of traditional gender roles.

Hitchcock's synergy with his collaborators didn't stop at his film crew. He also had longstanding partnerships with the actors and actresses he chose to work with. Notably, Cary Grant, James Stewart, and Grace Kelly were among his favorites, acting as extensions of Hitchcock himself in conveying his narratives on screen.

Films like "Rear Window", "Vertigo", and "North by Northwest" showcase James Stewart's range as an actor; Stewart impeccably portrays the flawed protagonists who embody Hitchcock's distinctive blend of suspense and dark human psychology.

Grace Kelly's icy, serene demeanor and vulnerable yet strong-willed performances made her a perfect muse for Hitchcock. Her performances in "Rear Window" and "To Catch a Thief" became a great influence on Hitchcock's later leading women.

Cary Grant, possibly Hitchcock's most frequent actor collaboration, brought to life roles that were often full of charm and charisma tinged with a sense of mystery and ambiguity. His performances in "North by Northwest" and "Notorious" are prime examples of this collaboration's success.

An essential synergy can also be found in Hitchcock's collaboration with graphic designer Saul Bass. His work on the opening sequences and poster designs of "Psycho", "Vertigo", and "North by Northwest" are truly works of art, contributing significantly to Hitchcock's visual narrative and aesthetic.

It's clear that Hitchcock didn't work in isolation. His collaborations were essential to his storytelling, proving that cinema is, indeed, a deeply intertwined, collaborative art.

These partnerships demonstrate not just a symbiotic bond between Hitchcock and his collaborators, but also show us the influence each had on one another. It's through these combined efforts that we get the cinematic masterpieces that Hitchcock is celebrated for.

The intricate themes and motifs, the unique suspenseful plots, the iconic characters—none of these would have been possible without Hitchcock's synergistic relationship with his collaborators. Their influence helped shape his art, refining it, and pushing the boundaries of what cinema could be.

Chapter 11: The Legacy of Fear

Threaded throughout Hitchcock's filmography, a lingering legacy of fear permeates each scene, from the tense anticipation that swells before a shocking reveal to the unnerving dread that lingers long after the credits roll. This legacy, undeniably influential, has roots in his masterful command of the language and techniques of cinematography. Hitchcock's ability to stoke and manipulate audiences' unease set a major precedent for the thriller genre. His audacious ideas, coupled with innovative technological adoption, continue to inspire contemporary directors, casting long shadows over modern cinema. Films like David Fincher's "Se7en," M. Night Shyamalan's "The Sixth Sense," and Jordan Peele's "Get Out" echo this influence, employing the Hitchcockian sense of escalating tension, making viewers squirm in their seats. Furthermore, his strategies carried weight beyond the genre lines, reshaping storytelling methods across various types of cinema. The enduring relevance of Hitchcock's thoughtful suspense, clever deception, and creative point-of-view shots makes his work not only timelessly impactful but also instructive for those learning the craft today. Thus, The Legacy of Fear is not only Hitchcock's gift to audiences worldwide but also to aspiring film students, serving as an awe-inspiring textbook on the art of suspenseful storytelling.

Hitchcock's Influence on Modern Cinema

With his innovative techniques and unique style, Alfred Hitchcock profoundly impacted modern cinema. From suspenseful thrillers to psychological dramas, his influence is evident in almost every genre. Let's delve deep into the impact of Hitchcock's work on contemporary filmmaking. Hitchcock's mark on the current film industry is impossible to ignore.

One of Hitchcock's most significant areas of influence is his distinct ability to craft suspense. Hitchcock's suspenseful storytelling can be seen replicated in films today such as "Paranormal Activity", "Jaws", and "The Ring". Directors of these films have taken cues from Hitchcock's slow build of tension, lingering shots, and ambiguous resolutions.

Moreover, Hitchcock's use of the 'MacGuffin', a plot device often utilized to propel the story, has become a standard storytelling technique in many modern films. For example, the 'Tesseract' in the Marvel Cinematic Universe or the 'Death Star plans' in Star Wars reflect Hitchcock's technique, driving the narrative while remaining somewhat elusive and mysterious.

Hitchcock's revolutionizing of perspectives is another key factor of his influence on modern cinema. He championed the use of point-of-view shots to give audiences a firsthand sense of the character's thoughts, feelings, and lived experiences, as we can see universally implemented across today's films.

Equally influential is Hitchcock's application of symbolism and metaphor, fostered through distinctive costume design and elements of mise-en-scène. Current films are suffused with subconscious visual cues that owe their heritage to Hitchcock's nuanced film language. The Nolan-directed "Inception", with its spinning top and Aronofsky's "Black Swan", with its feather motif, are just two examples.

Hitchcock was also a master manipulator of viewer emotions, using sound, lighting and innovative shot compositions to evoke specific responses. This manipulation of psychological response can be seen in modern films such as "Pulp Fiction". By blending unexpected visuals with a carefully designed soundscape, Hitchcock elicited strong emotions from his audiences, a technique which continues to be exploited in cinema to date.

Hitchcock's influence doesn't end with creative elements; he reshaped the very nature and perception of storytelling in film. His non-linear narrative design and intricate plot twists in "Vertigo" became something experimental filmmakers drew inspiration from, as exemplified clearly in the works of Christopher Nolan and David Fincher.

Another important aspect of Hitchcock's influence is his handling of suspense to explore and challenge societal norms and expectations. Vaunted auteurs such as Martin Scorsese have taken these thematic elements and incorporated them into their films, dealing with societal issues through the lens of suspense and drama.

Moreover, the innovative camera movements like the dolly zoom, which Hitchcock made famous in "Vertigo", changed the style of cinematic storytelling. This technique continues to be replicated in the modern era, with films like 'Jaws' using it to remarkable effect.

Directors like Brian De Palma and Steven Spielberg have often acknowledged Hitchcock's influence on their work. De Palma's "Carrie" is imbued with Hitchcock's psychological tension, while Spielberg has referenced Hitchcock's suspense-building technique numerous times in his body of work.

Hitchcock's unique depiction of women has also had a profound impact on how female characters are represented in modern cinema. His complex, intelligent, and independent female leads like those seen in "Rebecca" and "The Birds", were precursors to the many strong female protagonists we see in today's cinema.

It's not just directors who've been influenced by Hitchcock; composers and sound designers, too, owe a debt to the maestro of suspense. Hitchcock's partnership with composer Bernard Herrmann yielded some of the most exceptional scores in movie history, influencing how music is used in films even now.

The genius of Hitchcock can also be seen in the realm of television, with shows like "Bates Motel" and "The X-Files", where his motifs and visual techniques are evident. This exhibits the breadth of his influence, spanning from cinema to the smaller screen.

In summary, Hitchcock's influence on modern cinema is more potent now than ever before, with directors continuing to draw inspiration from his extensive catalogue of masterpieces. The suspense, the storytelling, the psychological underpinnings and the techniques pioneered by Hitchcock continue to define the landscape of contemporary cinema.

In conclusion, Hitchcock's contributions to cinema were seminal and had an undeniable influence on the stylistic and technical elements of modern filmmaking. His films remain required viewing for anyone seeking to understand the complexities and potential of contemporary cinema, as without Hitchcock, modern cinema could not exist as it does today. His legacy is a testament to his mastery, making him an enduring figure of fascination for filmmakers, scholars, and viewers alike.

Legacy on Modern Thrillers

The influence of Alfred Hitchcock's unique style on modern thrillers is both explicit and subliminal. From pioneering innovative cinematic techniques to crafting intricate narratives, he has significantly shaped how modern thrillers are conceived and viewed. His precise framing and impeccable pacing inspired a generation of filmmakers who endeavored to capture that same level of suspense and anticipation in their works.

The directors of penetrating thrillers such as "Silence of the Lambs," "Se7en," and "The Sixth Sense" have all shown an understanding of Hitchcock's ability to skillfully build tension. It's not a stretch to see the influence of Hitchcock's fingerprints in these films' memorable narratives and visually stunning scenes. Each one uses the camera to hint at hidden surprises or shocking revelations, a hallmark in many of Hitchcock's most revered films.

It's also important to note Hitchcock's influence on the reinterpretation of the genre. Directors have taken his approach and enhanced it, adding their personal touches, but the underlying principles remain Hitchcockian. This is particularly prominent in thrillers that focus on the psychological states of characters, delving deep into their motivations, fears, and obsessions.

Hitchcock's approach to storytelling, with its emphasis on suspense and visual storytelling, has helped redefine the thriller genre. Modern filmmakers, influenced by Hitchcock, often employ a robust narrative framework. They play with audience expectations, construct elaborate set pieces, and carefully modulate suspense, leading to a climax that may appear cathartic or unsettling based on the tone of the film.

The rise of neo-noir thrillers in recent decades also owes much to Hitchcock. To grasp this connection, look no further than Hitchcock's "Vertigo," replete with an obsessed protagonist, an intriguing mystery, and a distinct visual aesthetic. Films such as "Blade Runner" and "Mulholland Drive" contain elements of "Vertigo's" distinct style, fused with their singular visions, producing thrillers that both echo and expand upon Hitchcock's oeuvre.

The use of ambiguous characters and complex relationships, another Hitchcock staple, is a characteristic element in the thriller genre today. Hitchcock often presented characters with duplicitous natures, toying with the audience's judgments and emotions. This profound exploration of character complexity is vividly apparent in modern thrillers, captivating audiences with enigmatic figures that can't be readily classified as purely heroic or villainous.

Equally significant is Hitchcock's influence on the visual aesthetics of modern thrillers. His innovative use of camera techniques, including the famous "Vertigo" shot, is still widely applied today. Additionally, his use of light and shadow to create mood, tension, and mystery serves as inspiration in the visual construction of contemporary thrillers.

The inimitable soundscape of Hitchcock's thrillers, crafted with meticulous precision, has been impactful on the genre as well. Modern thrillers frequently employ intricate sound design to heighten suspense and create atmosphere, a nod to Hitchcock's enduring legacy.

Hitchcock's legacy has not only impacted the fundamental elements of thrilling storytelling but has also sought to consistently challenge and elevate the genre. His impact has been both broad and granular, shaping the genre's general direction while simultaneously influencing its micro-elements. From narrative structure to visual style, from character development to sound design - Hitchcock's imprints are deeply entrenched in the DNA of modern thrillers.

In conclusion, Hitchcock's enduring legacy on modern thrillers is an undeniable testament to his genius and his indelible contribution to the cinematic world. His body of work continues to serve as an invaluable source of inspiration, study, and passion for filmmakers and cineastes on how to craft riveting and compelling thrillers. It is no exaggeration to say that Hitchcock is not only the 'Master of Suspense' but also a master of legacy.

The Continuing Relevance

In an era where films are heavily reliant on special effects and fast-paced thrillers, the cinematic genius of Alfred Hitchcock continues to impress, intrigue and inspire. His timeless techniques and storytelling prowess remain highly influential, resonating in the works of contemporary filmmakers. In other words, the master of suspense isn't just a figure of the past — his relevance endures.

One key aspect of Hitchcock's enduring relevance is his visual storytelling. Hitchcock's films were not just viewed, but also felt, thanks to his unique ability to manipulate the audience's emotions through the use of visuals. Tools such as composition, lighting, and camera angles were used not only to narrate, but to stir feelings of suspense, fear, surprise and obsession. The power of visual language he wielded continues to be a significant area of study for film students and enthusiasts alike.

In an era where many films spell out everything for the audience, Hitchcock's portrayal of emotions and plot through atmospheric, visual storytelling remains refreshing. Today's filmmakers understand the value in this method and employ similar techniques to pull their viewers into the narrative rather than merely dictating the story to them.

Hitchcock's innovative narrative structures also continue to influence modern film. He subverted story rules to put his audience on the edge of their seats. His films played with plot conventions and expectations, often shattering norms and creating suspense in unpredictable ways. This approach to storytelling set Hitchcock apart in his time and continues to do so.

Though the impact of his unique narrative structures can be seen in numerous contemporary thrillers, the most evident is perhaps M. Night Shyamalan's films. Like Hitchcock, Shyamalan enjoys toying with plot conventions and keeping the audience guessing, pushing the envelope of suspense and fear, much to the delight of thriller aficionados.

In many ways, it's fair to say that the suspense-driven dread and intrigue that we often find in today's thrillers can be traced back to Hitchcock. While filmmakers may employ advanced technology and effects, the core tension-building techniques remain influenced by Hitchcock's approach.

In addition to his storytelling techniques, one of Hitchcock's major contributions to cinema was his unique style of characterization. He strayed from stereotypical herd-like characters to individuals with depth, complexity and uniqueness. Often, his characters exhibited a duality that reflected the inherent complexity of human nature. His villains were invested with a sense of charm or humanity, while his protagonists were flawed in some way.

Such nuanced characterization has become a norm in today's cinema. Filmmakers across genres understand and appreciate the value in creating multi-dimensional, relatable characters. The wave of anti-heroes and flawed yet loveable characters that we see in contemporary films speaks volumes about Hitchcock's influence.

No one can deny that Hitchcock also revolutionized the use of sound in films. His way of using sound and music to elevate suspense, provoke emotions, and even convey storyline is a common practice in films and series today. Looking at soundtracks from today's movies, we see several examples where sound is used to enhance storytelling in a manner that Hitchcock would have appreciated.

Adding to these points, the psychological underpinnings that made many of Hitchcock's works so resonant also continue to have an enduring appeal. He delved into phobias, guilt, obsessions, fragile mental states, all of which tapped into universal fears and insecurities. That exploration of psychological themes continues to captivate audiences and inspire filmmakers.

However, it's not just the thematic and stylistic elements that make Hitchcock's relevance enduring; it's also his consistency and the sheer volume of his work. With over fifty films to his name, each a learning resource in its own right, Hitchcock has left an invaluable treasure trove for filmmakers and academics to delve into.

This chapter has aimed to show just how enduring Hitchcock's influence is, his genius persisting across decades of cinematic evolution. His impact isn't limited to specific genres, branching out to influence a wide spectrum of films — from thrillers to dramas and beyond.

Perhaps what is most noteworthy is that even today, decades after his last film, his methods are not just being analyzed, but also actively utilized. This shows us that the art of cinema will always appreciate and find value in storytelling that can captivate its audience, regardless of the era it stems from. Hitchcock did this then, and if we pay mindfulness to it, we can see it happening now.

In conclusion, the techniques and conventions that Hitchcock pioneered still continue to shape the cinematic world. Even with the emergence of new cinematic tools and technologies, the essence of his craft continues to persist. From the structure and pacing of suspense, to the visual narration of storylines, to the character development and their intricate psychology, Hitchcock's influence cannot be overstated. It is his relentless innovation and craftsmanship that makes him not just a part of film history, but a continued inspiration for the future of filmmaking.

Conclusion

As we draw our exploration of Alfred Hitchcock's cinematography to a close, there are several key takeaways that should be underscored. First, Hitchcock's groundbreaking approach to film and his usage of techniques such as the MacGuffin, innovative sound concepts, and masterful framing have left an indelible mark in the realm of cinematography. His fearlessly experimental and prescient methods created a new language of visual storytelling that continues to inspire contemporary filmmakers.

Through our detailed examinations of his signature films such as "Psycho," "Vertigo," "The Birds," "Rear Window," and "North by Northwest," we've uncovered the sheer ingenuity of his craftsmanship. Each film serves as a time capsule, immortalizing his ability to maneuver the cinematic elements in ways that had never been done before, thereby creating a lasting influence on the landscape of cinema.

Furthermore, even the lesser-known gems like "Rope," "Strangers on a Train," and "Dial M for Murder" exhibit his unmistakable touch. Each film echoes his distinct style while showcasing the breadth and depth of his innovations within the scope of different storylines and themes.

We've also touched on Hitchcock's collaborations, exploring the symbiosis between him and his regular pool of actors, as well as writers and composers. These collaborations were instrumental in crafting masterpieces that encapsulated his vision, thus fostering a creative synergy that set new industry standards.

Most importantly, Hitchcock's legacy, which transcends the boundaries of time, is an ode to his mastery of suspense. As evidenced by our earlier discussions, his influence permeates the modern filmic landscape, seen not only in the genre of thriller, but also in dramas, comedies, and romance films alike.

His enduring relevance is a testament to his intuitive understanding of the dynamics of fear and suspense. Hitchcock expertly utilized cinema as a medium to delve into the primal human psyche, creating layered narrative experiences that captivated audiences then and now.

While this book has strived to elucidate the indispensable contributions of Hitchcock to the world of cinematography, it should serve as merely an initial foray into his vast, intricate, and immersive filmography. Hitchcock's work extends beyond the scope of this comprehensive guide, making him a fascinating subject of study for film lovers and scholars alike.

In conclusion, Hitchcock's evocative style, innovative techniques, and gripping narratives have etched his standing as one of the true masters of cinematography. His films are timeless works of art that engage, provoke, and delight viewers by defying expectations and pushing boundaries.

Understanding the depth and ingenuity of Hitchcock's work, equipped with the cinematographic concepts we've examined, allows for a renewed appreciation for the latent tension, dramatic irony, and haunting beauty in his films. This enhanced perception serves to enrich our understanding and enjoyment of cinematic storytelling.

As we delve deeper into the world of film, now enriched by a greater understanding of Hitchcock's legacy, let us remember his philosophy: "For me, the cinema is not a slice of life, but a piece of cake". True to Hitchcock's words, let's continue exploring the delicious, multi-layered world of the silver screen with newfound appreciation, seeking out the extraordinary within the ordinary, much like the master himself.

Appendix

In this appendix, we aim to provide an all-inclusive list of Alfred Hitchcock's works, a guide to relevant additional readings and viewings for those eager to further their understanding, and a comprehensive glossary of film terms used throughout the book. The combined knowledge found in this appendix will amplify your comprehension and appreciation of Hitchcock's cinematic universe.

Filmography

As a filmmaker, Alfred Hitchcock's prolific work spanned more than five decades, from silent films in the late 1920s to the sophisticated thrillers of the 1970s. His work comprises over 50 feature films, the majority of which have become classics in the world of cinema. Following is a chronological list of Hitchcock's significant works:

- The Lodger: A Story of the London Fog (1927)

- Blackmail (1929)

- The Man Who Knew Too Much (1934)

- The 39 Steps (1935)

- Rebecca (1940)

- Shadow of a Doubt (1943)

- Notorious (1946)

- Rope (1948)

- Strangers on a Train (1951)

- Dial M for Murder (1954)

- Rear Window (1954)

- Vertigo (1958)

- North by Northwest (1959)

- Psycho (1960)

- The Birds (1963)

- Marnie (1964)

- Frenzy (1972)

- Family Plot (1976)

Recommended Readings and Viewings

The following recommendations offer a deeper dive into the realm of Hitchcockian cinema. From biographies to critical essays, these sources provide information and analysis beyond the scope of this guide.

- Spoto, D. (1999). The Dark Side of Genius: The Life of Alfred Hitchcock.

- McGilligan, P. (2003). Alfred Hitchcock: A Life in Darkness and Light.

- Krohn, B. (2000). Hitchcock at Work.

- Films: "Hitchcock/Truffaut" (2015, Documentary), "The Making of Psycho" (1997, Documentary)

Glossary of Film Terms

This glossary includes critical film terms used throughout the book. It's designed to help you understand the language of cinematography and unlock the complexities behind Hitchcock's work.

1. *Angle:* The position of the camera in relation to the subject.

2. *Cut:* The switch from one shot to another.

3. *Depth of Field:* The range within which objects appear in sharp focus.

4. *Framing:* The arrangement of objects and performers within the boundaries of the film screen.

5. *MacGuffin:* A narrative element that drives the plot but is not significant in itself.

6. *Montage:* A sequence of shots assembled in a creative way to condense time, information and meaning.

7. *Pan:* A left or right rotational movement of the camera.

8. *Shot:* A single run of the camera.

9. *Zoom:* A shift in focal length that gives the illusion of moving closer or further away from the subject.

With this appendix in hand, you're well on your way to immersing yourself in the world of Hitchcock and appreciating his artistry in a brand-new light.

www.ingramcontent.com/pod-product-compliance
Lightning Source LLC
Chambersburg PA
CBHW031337060726
47590CB00007B/2503